the paradox
of
smoking

by

Richard L. Crowther

Directions/Publisher
P.O. Box 61135
Denver, CO 80206

Printed by:
A.B. Hirschfeld Press
Denver, Colorado

dedicated with deep concern for my wife Pearl and millions of others with respiratory and other diseases

Richard L. Crowther, FAIA has been engaged in architecture for over 40 years. His extensive architectural work deepened his concern about environmental quality and health. It was apparent that indoor air quality was of paramount importance to human well-being. It was equally apparent that smoking was a number-one factor of indoor air pollution. These concerns led to an in-depth research into constituents of tobacco smoke and its direct and indirect effects upon human vitality, health, and the interior of homes and buildings.

acknowledgments

The constructive participation of Robert Steimle is gratefully appreciated for his editing of text and research material.

Contributions of information from the American Lung Association and the American Cancer Society were most helpful.

The author wishes to thank the following people for their review and comments:

Robert A. Sandhaus, M.D., PhD. — senior staff physician, National Jewish Hospital/National Asthma Center; Assistant professor of medicine, University of Colorado Medical Center.

Martin Smith, Psy.D. — clinical psychologist, Behavior Therapy Institute of Colorado.

Lori Ohlson — holistic counselor and facilitator of nonsmoking clinics.

The author also wishes to thank Dr. Edward Martell, radiochemist at the National Center for Atmospheric Research in Boulder, Colorado, for his contribution of data on radon gas and radon daughters.

Drawings by the author.

the paradox of smoking
Richard L. Crowther, FAIA

table of contents

table of contents continued

prologue

Perhaps the irrationality of fuming tobacco between two receptive lips has added to its social tolerance. Everyone loves a good enigma and a compelling paradox.

Every fragment of life has been saturated with tobacco smoke. While no one (except the tobacco industry and its more addicted adherents) extols smoking, it remains condoned and condemned in society, business, government, economics, and religion, as well as in architecture and its interiors.

This book explores a range of interim and more substantive means and measures to lessen the harm for smoker and nonsmoker alike. This is not a "how to quit" book, but rather a look at this pervasive and persuasive habit.

Smoking can be a formidable obstacle to interpersonal, intimate, and transactional human relationships. The question is what love and affection is lost by the fumes of a cigarette or tobacco breath? What anger displaces amicable relationships because a partner, a friend, or an acquaintance smokes? What transactions go down the drain because of offensive smoking? What sales are lost because a salesperson lights up? What job opportunities fade away for the applicant that smokes?

Smoking has no positive aspects. It is a serious drug habit. By any terms of judgment smoking results in a quagmire of behavior. It is a habit difficult to break. It most seriously affects everyone.

the paradox of smoking

From times historic, humans have sought to lessen the intolerable as well as to gratify their existence with various mediators. Smoking is an oral, expressive, sensual, territorial, and palliative mediator. On the other side of the coin, it is toxic, addictive, odoriferous, intrusive, and incendiary.

Its oral and manipulative manifestations are an expressive body language. In a state of habituation the cigarette, cigar, or pipe becomes part of the smoker. In a state of addiction the person becomes part of the cigarette, cigar, or pipe. The addicted individual is caught in the web of psycho-oral behavior and biophysical dependency. Smoking is sensual to the smoker but is repulsive to most non-smokers and a certain number of smokers. The smoker's feeling of personal-territorial expandibility accompanies visual drifts of smoke that become an annoying intrusion to others. In the mind of the smoker, the ignited tobacco appears to level acute anxiety and apprehensions and increase the ability to cope. However, smoking raises the apprehension and anxiety level of the nonsmoker and addiction can considerably raise the stress level of the smoker.

Toxic chemicals and radioactivity poison the smoker and others in range. The odoriferous outpourings from cigarette, cigar, or pipe breach the personal space of others and contaminate their hair, clothes, lungs, and possessions. The indoor environment is not spared from sticky, odoriferous residues. Tobacco smoking is more addictive and broadly harmful than illegalized heroin. A trail of burns, scorches, and fires follows the smoking syndrome.

A simple evaluation of the foregoing is that smoking as a common habit is an inescapable enigma. However, in the land of human affairs, enigmas can develop into first rate paradoxes. Compounding the reality of smoking is a bevy of other realities.

The constituents of tobacco and tobacco smoke fall into the drug category and yet no federal agency evaluates, regulates, or compels the disclosure of ingredients, the amount of dosage, nor the dispensing thereof. Although tobacco products are more nefarious and lethal than many other products, no government agency in reasonable measure protects the young, the old, the ill, or the healthy by supervised point of sale of the products and from all forms of tobacco advertising. The province of laws and regulations is to protect the health, safety, and welfare of citizens. Such protection is grossly inadequate in regard to cigarettes, cigars, pipes, snuff, and chewing tobacco.

Another paradox is that businessmen for the most part make no distinction between hiring smokers or non-smokers. Absenteeism, lost productivity, annoyance, irritation and harm to others, documents, furnishings and all interior surfaces plus cleaning up the mess costs lots of money. A simple question is why does not the employer make the smoker pay in less compensation or other means for the smoker's indulgence? A second question is why is smoking not controlled in every business, work, or gathering place?

The most profound paradox occurs at the home and social level. Smokers love their children, their spouse, and others and yet in their home and car or that of others, most often they spew their odoriferous smoke around regardless of discomfort, irritation, and harm. Nice, loving, considerate parents, friends, and acquaintances that smoke in indoor spaces where others are gathered leave in question those more notable attributes of character.

the habit is a worrisome thing

the pervasive habit

If smoking were not such a pervasive indulgence it might
be ignored. The pungent habit attracts the human mind
and body to experiment and bear the guise of another
state of being. Smokers and ex-smokers are not like persons who have never smoked. They have felt and know
their beguiling capture by habituation, addiction, and their
smoker's mind, that is, a mental attitude that consciously
and/or unconsciously accompanies the smoking habit.
The image of the smoking syndrome is literally imprinted
into the network of the brain. The persistence of memory
intimately stimulates the smoker to continue the habit
and challenges the ex-smoker in the unguarded moment
to return to the habit.

It is frightful that an innocuous start into the habit can
end with such devastating consequences. Once beyond
the body's revulsion to the inhalation of the acrid fumes a
stoic mental accommodation takes over into what is per-
ceived as a smoker's pleasure.

Our society has posted no vivid warning, no effective roadblock, nor succinct descriptions strong enough to prevent newcomers from ascribing to the habit or if habituated or addicted from imbibing in cigarettes, cigars, pipes, snuff, or chewing tobaccos. The package and advertising warning, "The Surgeon General has determined that cigarette smoking is dangerous to your health," has little meaning by its very repetition. Besides, who has really seen a picture of the Surgeon General or has a reliable impression of what his function is? The message sounds like the hollow voice of authority but acts as a legal protector for the tobacco industry against liability claims.

The label also ignores everyone else who doesn't smoke. The label should include that smoking injures the vitality and health of others exposed to it.

Smoking, by any definition, negates wholesome values. According to the American Lung Association, 90 percent of smokers want to quit the habit. Once addicted, the realization of the nefarious harm of smoking creates the personal paradox of someone mentally seeking to defend their habit while ardently hoping to stop it.

A number one question is how to dig into the industry that extols its death-dealing products, hands out free samples, seeks to penetrate market segments, and tries to hook men, women, and youth into the addictive web of smoking. The tobacco industry is as insidious as its products.

Above and beyond the heavily documented and observed harm to health, the cigarette, cigar, and pipe are the greatest polluters of indoor air, major cause of burns, scorches, and fires as well as a heavy burden to clean up the spent tobacco mess and clean and restore interior surfaces contaminated with the viscous brown residues.

Smoking is pervasive at every public and private level. Even the majority of smokers favor that smoking be reasonably controlled in public places. We all pay a heavy economic toll for this social intrusion upon health, property, and environment. There are few limits as to where, what, or how often most persons can smoke within the confines of indoor space.

The complex chemical components emanating from countless cigarettes, cigars, and pipes inundate the realm of breathable air with pervasive, harmful, radioactively charged particulates, poisonous gasses, and toxic effluents. The volumetric enclosure of indoor space usually with neither adequate filtration nor ventilation impounds the smoke and captures the sticky residues on every interior surface, including people.

a little history

The tobacco plant is native to the Western Hemisphere, but it has played different roles in many cultures, roles ranging from the medicinal to the monetary. American Indians used it in religious and other ceremonies. In 1492, Columbus sighted not only the New World but native Indians engrossed in smoking rolled leaves and the pipes that they called "tobacco,"[1] the term Europeans applied to the plant, which was cultivated and used throughout the Americas. The Mexican Indians believed the plant cured asthma, bronchitis, and rheumatism![2]

This idea spread with the plant (for example, it was used by men, women, and children in London against the Plague) as, first medicinally and then socially, tobacco smoking, sniffing, and chewing became very popular throughout Europe — and very unpopular. James I is the most famous antismoking activist because of his 1604 "Counterblaste to Tobacco"[3] and his taxation of the "Precious stink."[4] Innocent XII excommunicated anyone using

---

[1] C.A. Johnson, "Talk About Tobacco and Snuff."

[2] Ibid.

[3] Ott, Joseph K, " 'Soverane Weed' Artifacts Betwitch Tobaccomaniacs," *Denver Post,* Dec. 1978.

[4] Ibid.

tobacco in St. Peters. In Russia, smokers' lips were slit and snuffers' noses removed.[5] Despite these ambitious enactments against the noxious weed, its use spread around the world with colonialism. As religions encountered it, some forbade it; in recent times, an increasing number of sects are adopting no-smoking positions.[6] In the New World, tobacco growing and the growing use of smoking materials continued nearly unabated.

By the eighteenth century, pipe and cigar smoking had gained social standing, but cigarettes were held in low regard (having been created by beggars in Spain by wrapping spent cigar butts in paper).[7] In 1869, fewer than two million hand-rolled cigarettes were produced in the United States, and by the early 1870s, per-capita tobacco consumption had been falling for a century.[8] The economic crisis of 1873, milder tobacco varieties, improved curing methods, and machine rolling in the 1880s made cigarettes attractive to more people.[9] The "improved" curing methods made the smoke "milder"; i.e., more acid than alkaline. Alkaline smoke, such as from pipes and cigars, is too harsh to be inhaled, and less of the nicotine in the tobacco enters the body more slowly through the mucous membranes of the mouth.[10] The acid smoke of cigarettes, however, is mild enough to enter the lungs without irritating the smoker, and the nicotine can go directly through the bloodstream and the heart to the brain, eliciting a rapid nicotine response that is highly addictive. In 1889, two and one-half billion cigarettes were sold in the United States.

With the rapid growth of the movie industry since 1900, the cigarette, cigar, and pipe became familiar and con-

---

[5] Ibid.

[6] George W. Cornell, "Foes of Smoking Making Battle Religious Issue," *Denver Post,* 1983.

[7] Edward de Bono, ed., *Eureka! An Illustrated History of Inventions from the Wheel to the Computer* (New York: Holt, Rinehart and Winston, 1974), p. 107.

[8] William Bennett, "The Cigarette Century," *Science 80,* Sept.-Oct., 1980, pp. 37-43.

[9] Bono, 107.   [10] Bennett, p. 40.

venient props for the Hollywood filmmaker. This cultural example was powerful, as idols of the screen appeared to enjoy and need the soothing manipulation of a cigarette, cigar, or pipe. The cultural idiom of smoking was further strengthened by its identity with sexual, social, and leisure pursuits. Today, peer pressure amplifies the stress for social compliance in our complex society, and personal insecurities are strong inducements for people to smoke.

changing times

The tide has turned from a complacency about smoking. A swing is occurring from social acceptance to nonacceptance. These value judgements about smoking in public places are formed to a large extent by changing perceptions about the harm of smoking upon the nonsmoker and smoker. The mainstream thought of acceptable behavior filters down through various responsive individuals to where it becomes a social custom or prevailing social state of mind.

Smoking has historically undergone a recurrent pattern of acceptance and rejection. Today, a preponderance of evidence brings into sharper focus the extenuating harm from tobacco smoking. It is clear that it debilitates the vitality, composure, and well-being of everyone. Smoking hangs on tenaciously because of its compulsive and relapsing type of addiction. It is the greatest common social offender. It is a habit often intolerable to the smoker as much as the nonsmoker. It destroys physical and economic health and well-being. Tobacco smoking is an enslavement by its pernicious effect upon the smoker and nonsmoker. What is good or bad is important to society. Who can doubt that tobacco smoking, chewing, or sniffing is bad?

Underscoring the changing public feelings towards smoking, a national survey of attitudes about smoking (recently released by the American Lung Association) has doc-

8

umented for the first time that a majority of Americans — both smokers and nonsmokers — now believe that smokers should refrain from smoking in the presence of nonsmokers. The survey, conducted by the Gallup Organization, showed that 82 percent of nonsmokers and 55 percent of current smokers agree smokers should not light up around nonsmokers.

The survey also revealed that two-thirds of smokers believe involuntary (passive) smoking is hazardous to the health of nonsmokers. The results of the survey are summarized below.[1]

Smokers Should Refrain From Smoking in the Presence of Nonsmokers (%)

	Agree	Disagree	No Opinion
Smokers	55	39	6
Nonsmokers	82	14	4
Former Smokers	70	22	8

Smoking Is Hazardous to the Health of Nonsmokers (%)

	Agree	Disagree	No Answer
Smokers	64	30	6
Nonsmokers	84	11	5
Former Smokers	80	15	5

Smoking Is Harmful to Your Health (%)

	Agree	Disagree	No Opinion
All Respondents	92	5	3

[1] Data adapted from information provided by the American Lung Association in New York.

smoking is a tough rut

the smoker's paradox

Smoking is an oral and breathing event. As explained by Lori Ohlson, an ex-smoker and a consultant in human values and relationships, the inhalation of tobacco smoke focuses awareness on the breathing process. The sensation of the inhalation and exhalation of the smoke acts as an emotional mediator. It pacifies the senses and takes the brunt off anger, frustration, and loss of confidence. Smoking acts as a suppressor of errant emotions.

As breathing may make a person feel alive, smoking inhalation becomes its sensory replacement. The oral contact with cigarette, cigar, or pipe as well as an inner dependency on smoke-filled respiratory cavities provides a supportive gratification. It is a habit that appeals to brain sensation but ignores, deludes, or challenges brain logic. The addictive and supportive inducement of smoking is so great that there is little wonder that for most individuals it is a tenacious habit to break.

The question is what self-reinforcing gratifications, readily obtainable and socially acceptable, are available that can compete with the persistent effects of tobacco indulgence? This question is personal and individual, as it goes to the root of intimate values. The paradox is that smokers smoke to sustain self-value and feeling of being while suffering a harmful de-valuing of body and mind by the act of smoking. If we value fresh, pure air, or want the love of someone who cannot abide our smoking, or can find an intense living pleasure in wholesome pursuits, we can learn to acquire that which is higher (vitality, health, freedom) over that which is lower (addiction, loss of vitality, and self-indulgence).

It is seldom that smokers stop smoking simply by logic. Feelings and emotions must accompany motivations. To halt the habit, the smoker must experience a rebirth or at least a new realization of self.

Most smokers want to end their ingrained indulgence, but how to shed the smoking habit that has become part of their thinking, feeling, and emotional being can be inexorably difficult. There is always the inner hope that as they continue to smoke they will stop tomorrow, or tomorrow, or tomorrow.

Gestalt psychology reflects the *now*. How, *now* can the smoker change a life-style? Books, classes, clinics, physicians, psychologists, friends, family, clergy, group, and health organizations all have or can have an influence on motivations and ways and means of quitting the habit — but the real need *and desire* to quit lies within the individual. Smoking remains a compulsive paradox.

smoking and stress

Stress is the great American malady. From the nuclear dilemma to local stresses, our neural, physical, and mental capacities bear an overwhelming weight. Inability to cope with the escalations of stress keeps smokers smoking.

For the smoker the question is always when does smoking itself become a contributor to instead of a detractor from external and inner personal tensions? Watching a chain-smoker conveys a poignant impression that smoking is a relentless, inner stress.

Regardless of the feelings of relief from the weight of anxiety, frustration, or other tensions, the smoker always carries the mental burden of his or her own habit. Despite the mental exercise of denial, smokers are well aware that smoking is harmful to them. However, this knowledge is most often suppressed and is not part of conscious awareness. How many smokers know and inwardly feel that they are casting stenchful tobacco odors and annoying, irritating, and harmful smoke upon others is open to statistical evaluation.

The fact is that smoking as to place, intensity, and type of tobacco, places a definitive neural, mental, and physical stress upon others. Indoors in public and private places there is literally no escape from the pungent, all-pervasive fumes. Retreat to a smokeless indoor space or to the great, all-absorbing outdoors can be the only way an escapee (nonsmoker or smoker) can find a breathable refuge.

By any measure smoking is an intensive, stress-inducing pastime. The stress is psychoneural, psychologic, physiologic, and downright costly!

body and mind

In this physical world we only get one body and mind. It is a magnificent organism of sensations, thought response, and adaption to the ever-changing conditions of our environment. To contaminate or injure this scope of mind and body beautiful seems like a travesty against the course of nature.

We have a brief span of years. In this span most of us would like to have a full and productive life. Conditions of the environment, our fortunes within the scenario of living, and how we treat our body and mind determine the health and tranquility of our being.

Imbibing on the burning leaves of tobacco and the additives and wrapper of a cigarette results in congestion and devitalization of our oral, visual, and pulmonary passages; impairment of the heart; vasoconstriction of our blood vessels; damage and irritation to the eyes; staining of the teeth, fingers, nails; and, exacerbation of the skin.

Not only is the smoker drawn into the biologic habituation and addiction of smoking, but everyone within contained indoor space is made subject in measure to the poisonous, airborne toxins. Smoking does not add one cubit to the value of life but takes many cubits away.

It is strange how the indirection of body and mind into the choreography of smoke trails as well as attitudinal positioning of cigarette, cigar, or pipe became a manner of visual aesthetics. Unfortunately, the long-term vitriolic effects upon vigor of breathing and vitality belie the social mannerism.

The scene can be one of young, well-dressed, handsome men and beautiful women cavorting in a delight of social pleasure. The printed full-color ad that depicts this scene does not reveal the putrid smell of cigarettes, carcinogenic fumes invading the lungs of smoker and smokee

13

(nonsmoker next to smoker), or stink residing in hair, clothes, skin, and all soft luxuries of indoor furnishings. Hidden among the players are the burns and scorches upon carpet and furniture, with a few holes added to personal attire.

**without smokes
i'm free as
a bird**

ˎfreedom

Most smokers would like to be free of their habit. Non-smokers share this wish to an even greater degree. The burning question is how can the smoker be free from habit enslavement and the nonsmoker encourage and aid the smoker towards cessation?

It is curious that many women smoke "macho" cigarettes. Perhaps they are trying to buy identity, esteem, and confidence, clearly depicted by the Marlboro man and Camel smoker. Curiously these brands are touting the "lights" rather than heavy tobacco.

The basic name of the game is how the cigarette manufacturers can keep the enslavement going and how the smoker can escape from the addiction. The name of the package, the identifying message, the ambience of the ad are all worked out with adroit and contentious effort in the cloister of the cigarette advertising agency. How to bait, hook, and catch the unsuspecting female or male is an interesting venture.

The cigarette industry wants to freely savor full saturation advertising. The heavily addicted (generally) want the freedom to smoke any amount, anywhere. The light smoker (generally) would like to have some breathable air. The nonsmoker would like a full snoot-full of fresh air at any time.

Freedom is thus how we define it. If no smoking occurred anywhere or was not allowed anywhere we would all be free of the attributes of the smoke-filled air. Thus is it not that any amount of smoking in measure destroys the freedom of the smoker and nonsmoker alike?

the price of enjoyment

Any indulgence of life can become a gratification for someone. Any facet of life can qualify as a possible indulgence. Suzy may have an indulgence in fried beans. Don may have an indulgence in motorcycle racing.

Whatever, and wherever, humans seek out gratifications: large, small, harmful, nonharmful, expensive, and inexpensive. Cutting out paper dolls or blowing soap bubbles can be a big turn on at low cost.

The name of the game in life seems to be how to get some enjoyment. Unfortunately, from an early age we discover that enjoyment may have some drawbacks. The drawback might be in the loss of affection or goodwill of others, a loss or burden in money, or that it hurts our health or messes up our person and surroundings.

Indulgences can serve as a bulwark against depression,

as a reinforcement of being, or as a means of being physically and mentally occupied. It seems that man "cannot live by bread alone," but needs an indulgence. Women are literally wrapped up in the same compulsions.

Indulgence requires opportunity, in money and/or availability, the motivation to indulge, the cultural, social, and personal impression of the indulgence, and the promise of gratification offered by it.

The question is when does an indulgence become a habituation, a partial addiction, or an absolute craving? "I gotta have it!" our mind and body can shout with overwhelming power.

On a scale of enjoyment without negative increments, smoking would score somewhere around zero. What is so compelling about so harmful a pastime that over 50 million Americans indulge in it?

Along with the hard-line indulgences that can lead to heavy addiction, smoking can well be equated with excessive imbibing of alcohol, marijuana, cocaine, heroin, and other mind-boggling and destructive compulsive behavior.

The question in life is how can we neatly prioritize our indulgences and compulsions to delight with little or no harm to ourselves, to others, to the environment, or to our pocketbook (or that of others)?

time

When time hangs heavy or conversely, when anxiety races with time, smokers are apt to smoke more. Smoking seems more in phase with idle time than action time.

Smoking is antagonistic to participant sports, in contrast to spectator bench polishing. Even downhill a runner would not do well puffing on a cigarette, cigar, or pipe. Smokers generally are visibly short-winded in any encounter with exertion through time.

Time and *interval* exposure to volumes of inhaled tobacco smoke are the final monitor on length of life. Everyone doesn't succumb equally, genetically. We are all different with different inbuilt immunities and organic resistance.

Time even hangs heavier on mind and body when we suffer from demanding malaise. Cancer, emphysema, heart disease, or arteriosclerosis bear the weight of anxiety, fear, pain, and time.

The most imperative function that we have through time is breathing. We can go without food for days, without water for hours, but without breathing for only minutes. Breathing is the metronome of our body. We experience the world in rhythms to our breathing and metabolic pressures.

Smoking impairs the flow of these functions and distorts the perception of those addicted.

Time spent in smoking subtracts time from our lives. It subtracts it from the nonsmoker as well as the smoker. The ostensible time, money, and human vitality wasted in earning, buying, lighting, puffing, clean up, maintenance, repair, contention, well-being, health, guilt, and days of life for everyone should defy most attractions of the habit.

the spectrum of a habit

There is a tendency to lump smokers together in one pot
and nonsmokers in another. Actually for each there are
all gradations in between. There are nonsmokers who
have never smoked, nonsmokers who tried a time or two
to smoke, nonsmokers who smoked lightly at interspersed
times, ex-smokers who were habituated, ex-smokers who
were addicted, light smokers, moderate smokers, and
heavy smokers still smoking. Somewhere in this scale
each person will find himself or herself, as well as relatives,
friends, and acquaintances. It is this very diffuse continuum in human attitude and behavior that has allowed
smoking to persist as a social element.

There is a greater consideration in differentiating between types of smokers than types of nonsmokers. Smoking is a more visible and impressive act than nonsmoking.
Chain smoking is an apogee of attention. It is a display of
an arrogant domination over a self in ultimate submission.

The nonsmoker who has never smoked is far removed
from the sensory cravings of the deeply addicted smoker.
In contrast, the reformed smoker can be a tough crusader
against smoking. The average middle-of-the-road nonsmoker can be placid and unbelievably tolerant as
smokers light up on every hand and obscure vision of
anything within 20 feet.

Observance of individual traits and behavioral responses
at any level of human restraint or excess defies hard-line
conclusions. Nevertheless, the more we understand
human nature, the better we can deal with it.

no smoking is uplifting

not to start

If no one started to smoke and as the smoking population shortened its own life, we could enjoy being indoors with more breathable air. How to stop the start requires more public concern and involvement. The American Lung Association has active school programs to dissuade the young from starting a habit which at some point they may not be able to stop. Stop smoking clinics and programs abound but so low a number (under 20 percent) of smokers remain as ex-smokers. Smoking is so addictive that a *massive* effort is needed to keep youth and adults from being freshly caught in the net of the habit.

Not to start has a hollow meaning unless the inducements to start are eliminated or are outflanked. How to outflank the peers of youth as well as the respected adult who smokes, eliminate or control smoking in public and private places, prohibit all forms of tobacco product advertising, and stop the open sale of cigarettes in dispensing machines remains a question.

smoking segregation

Every building is a multi-chambered container. Within each contained space walls, ceilings, and floors intercept airborne cigarette, cigar, and pipe-tobacco smoke. Within each contained space people live, eat, work, and play.

A declining dimension of indoor space concentrates the density of smoke. It is analogous to the fish in a small fishbowl. There is less air and more smoke to breathe as the indoor space becomes smaller. There is less opportunity for avoidance or escape from the lethal fumes of ignited tobacco.

A singular benefit for the smoker in a small contained space is that it can be provided, furnished, and separately situated at less initial and subsequent operating costs than a larger indoor space. On the other side of the coin a small, contained space can be provided for the nonsmoker as an escape from smoking in other parts of a building. It is obviously necessary to designate by sign or symbol that the chamber is specifically for either smoking or nonsmoking.

The manipulations to separate smokers and nonsmokers suggest the racial/social segregation that we have tried ardently to put behind us. The striking difference is that providential segregation of smoking and nonsmoking indoor spaces spells emotional, health, and environmental freedom for smoker and nonsmoker alike.

In contrast racial, religious, or social congregation and mixing conveys no health, biologic, or practical harm.

Smoking segregation was practiced during our period of passenger railroading, in elite clubs, and private offices in the 1880s through the 1920s. In evidence were smoking cars, club rooms, and the private business offices at that time. Smoking was not accepted in the majority of offices, institutions, or homes. The erosion of reasonable social demarcation as to smoking was surreptitiously aided and abetted by the tobacco industry.

The very word "segregation" in human terms has a negative ring but with so injurious, devitalizing, and pervasive an addiction as smoking, it is a most reasonable, considerate, and beneficial strategy. "Do unto others as you would have them do unto you," is a thought appropriate to the circumstance of smoking.

cigarettes spoil my taste buds

salt, sugar, caffeine, and tobacco

It is difficult to draw the line between habituation and addiction. Perhaps the distinction is that habituations can be stopped with some degree of ease while addictions cannot.

Whether habituation or addiction, there appears to be a growing renunciation of salt, sugar, and caffeine in the interests of better health. Statistics appear to confirm this public wisdom.

The use of tobacco in habituation and addiction in all of its forms is becoming less socially acceptable. The swing of smokers to low-tar, low-nicotine, and filtered cigarettes indicates a striving towards health.

Unfortunately tobacco is burned, not eaten, and general

studies indicate that the filtertip, low-tar varieties do not represent a crusade for health.

The word "natural" is used for marketing magic. Salt, sugar, caffeine, and tobacco are all natural but they all have adverse effects on the human constitution. On a scale of 1 (high) to 10 (low) in biologic harm, it is likely that smoking would be a 1. Smoking is the number-one indoor polluter, number-one cause of cancer, respiratory and heart disease, number-one in burns and fires, and number-one as the most deplored of common addictions.

Individuals seem to be more successful in cutting down or quitting the use of salt, sugar, and caffeine than the use of tobacco. Tobacco has over 3,600 chemical constituents. Many are biologically poisonous as well as radioactively harmful. This injurious complexity of smoking exists in sharp contrast to the ingestion of salt, sugar, and caffeine.

While it seems appropriate that harmful edibles be eliminated or drastically reduced, smoking fails to elicit the proportional attention and concern that it should.

lessons in time

In this world we are given only a limited span of years in which to witness our reasonably predicted as well as unpredicted tides of fortune. Within our life span we may look into the past as the future unfolds and compare what is happening now with what we thought would happen.

In the late 1920s large outdoor billboards illustrated a man with a cigarette in hand. The next painting of the billboard showed a woman admiringly looking at the man. After a number of months, another painted panel had the woman saying, "Blow some my way." In the next subsequent panel (after more months of time), the woman was illustrated directly holding a cigarette. This subtle transfer of the cigarette from male to female remains indelibly in my memory. It continues to this day that women remain a marketing target of cigarette companies.

In comparison, the screenplays of Hollywood (as near as we know) made no *conscious* attempt to subvert the moviegoer's mind and body into the smoking habit. However, within the play, cigarettes, cigars, and pipes as symbolic props amenable to an actor's role did more to indoctrinate public acceptance than could be singly accomplished by the tobacco promoters.

Time marches on and we are both boldly and subtly indoctrinated by everything that surrounds us. Unless we can clearly perceive what is indoctrinating us and its possible effect upon our future, we impair our human spirit and what the future will have in store for us. A constant introspection is needed over events and matters as they occur, with timely counteractions taken, to protect us from collective harm. "An ounce of prevention is worth a pound of cure" is an appropriate adage.

**for us twosome
puffin' is gruesome**

skin deep

Everyone would like to be attractive. Although women are expected to beguile men with their beauty, men share sufficient sexual and ego-centered vanity to "look their best."

Except for head, neck, arms, and possibly legs, for the most part our bodies are clothed through most human encounters and transactions. Only the revelation of the beach or locker room exposes more wrinkles, hair, and color of the naked skin.

It is easy to pick out most consistent smokers by the odor of their clothes, hair, breath, skin, and often the yellow staining of fingers, fingernails, and teeth. Such additions to the human body do not for beauty make. The lingering odors from tobacco smoke or the strong para- lyzing fragrance used to cover the obnoxious residues do not invite close companionship.

Cosmetics, lotions, and perfumes are sold by the ton in the U.S. presumably to make the person more appealing.

It is a paradox that any self-respecting person seeking sensual delights would puff on a stenchful, burning weed and furthermore, that they would pay to do it and might pay to cover it up.

New cigarettes are designed to be more attractive as well as the package that contains them. Does it not seem a shame to destroy the designer's effort by tearing the package apart and burning up his handiwork?

Various aromatics have been introduced into tobacco mixtures. Some recent cigarettes smell like an aromatic, pipe-tobacco blend. As an oral substitute for smoking, why not sanitized tubes through which to inhale delicate organic fruit aromas (uncontaminated by additives, pesticides, or synthetic fragrances)? Such addiction might be one of supreme delight!

the paradox continues

Religious and meditative circles strive for purity of body and soul. Smoking appears inimical to a state of blissful purity with its heavy stench and irritating constituents. It is a curious enigma and paradox that smoking is not banned by more religions rather than the few who do.

On the front of justice and order, smoking still prevails in closeted jury rooms. Those who determine the fate of others can find themselves subject to an assault by smoking. Has any defendant been unjustly incarcerated by jurors eager to escape from a smoke-filled jury room?

Licensed architects and engineers, as defenders of human health and well-being, determine the state of the indoor environment. Smoking prevails in indeterminate amounts in almost all public and private indoor spaces. The enigma and paradox is that the architectural enclosure and space planning ventilation and filtration systems are rarely planned or designed to meet the on-slaught of indoor smoking.

There is a human proclivity to create soft, yielding interiors for comfort of body and mind. Seldom is thought that the fetid outpourings of the cigarette, pipe, or cigar are critically absorbed into the fluffy fibers. There the odor lingers, waiting for the next attack of odors.

The last and most mind-provoking paradox is of the tobacco industry itself. It proclaims its deep, heartfelt concerns. It clearly acclaims the unmatched benefits of smoking, versus the industry's version of those vitriolic attacks against the habit.

advertising

Advertising can be a powerful force for good or powerful force for bad. Often an advertising agency neither knows nor is in a position to judge the product they extol, nor do they care about its real merits.

Most people do not believe that advertising has a controlling effect on their lives. Most people believe in their own independent and free will. In their mind, they make the choice. To a large extent this is likely to be true, but they are not immune from external influence.

However, when advertising promotes or sustains the bad, it becomes an insidious sustainer of the idea that the bad is not so bad. Cigarette advertising with its saturation and market-segment techniques is an example par excellence of a bad. Such agencies should win the gold medal for lifting the bad into the light of the good.

**in the whole world –
why smoke here?**

the hospital scene

Hospitals are a notable paradox as to the matter of smoking. In most hospitals there is no separation in the main lobby and waiting areas between smokers and nonsmokers. Patients in the rooms usually fare better particularly if a nonsmoker is adamant in not being cooped in with a smoker.

The really curious aspect is that cigarette machines and gift shops that sell cigarettes generally prevail. A comment is that these make money. Such is true, and the hospital already makes money from the addicts who struggle with various and sundry tobacco-related infirmities. On the other hand, thoughtful and concerned doctors patently (sometimes even strongly) advise their smoke-injured patients to quit the habit.

As to the smoking patient, the question is whether such a person can fare better with or without the habit when under the stress of surgery or other hospital treatment. It is unlikely that any other patients will welcome or prosper with smoke-laden air.

Another matter is fire. If a few bedsheets get burns or get scorched that is one thing, a real fire is another with many patients not in an ambulatory condition. Oxygen often presents another level of hazard as do linen rooms and other concentrations of flammables. A happier state of mind would exist for any contemplative person who is bedridden if smoking were not permitted by patients, staff, guests, or anyone else in the hospital confines. A separate smoking lounge, separately ventilated and competely closed off and equipped with a fire detection device and fire sprinkler and with noncombustible furniture and furnishings is a cautious answer to the lack of such a facility. Shouldn't such a provision be mandatory?

pain and death

Smoking substantially increases the probability of suffering from the more painful diseases and a more painful death. Not only has it been documented that smokers experience more pain than nonsmokers under similar circumstances, but an addiction can lead to more intense smoking under conditions of painful anxiety.

Death is inevitable for all of us. However, smoking hastens the likelihood of diseases that result in earlier death. No cigarette is a safe cigarette. No cigar or pipe is free from causing physical harm.

An old adage, "every cigarette is a nail in your coffin," has gone unheeded despite the ever-mounting evidence that smoking, indeed, enhances the probability of an earlier death.

After a visit to those who suffer from the anxiety-ridden, painful, and ever-torturous maladies caused by smoking, perhaps those youth, those beautiful ladies, and attractive men might be dissuaded from starting or encouraged to give up the tenacious habit. Some persons who were physically unable to smoke with oral cancer have been seen to smoke through a tracheotomy performed so that they might breathe. Inveterate heavy smokers often deny that smoking can hurt anyone or that a chronic malignant or cardiovascular disease might have been caused by their habit.

smoking airways

A commercial aircraft is a pressurized tube with wings jetting through space. A passenger who is a nonsmoker or smoker sits in the seat of the flying tube with some possible restrained anxiety. While smoking appears to lessens the smoker's anxiety, it most likely increases the nonsmoker's anxiety. For passengers who think, the question is what happens in an onboard fire emergency and it isn't safe to drop the oxygen masks? The FAA estimates that a flashfire will race through a plane in 90 seconds and that passengers could exit from the plane in 90 seconds. Of course, at 30,000 feet altitude and with highly toxic, combustible seats and other interior fittings, the question becomes substantially enlarged. The FAA proposes restrictive standards that would convert existing and new aircraft to a more noncombustible interior status, over a probable period of three to five years. Meanwhile, if smoking were prohibited in planes, a major source of accidental fire would be eliminated.

Pre-flight assigned seats condemn a nonsmoking passenger to incalculable tobacco-smoke drift and indeterminable amounts of intrusive smoke. Everyone is not in the best of health, or can be elderly or a child. Should even a healthy person be subjected to the odoriferous, toxic, and clinging fumes from airborne smoke inside the restricted space of the cabin?

If the smoker had to pay a substantial extra monetary tariff to sit in the smoking section, would most smokers elect to smoke or not to? How much above the regular fare would make most smokers not smoke aboard the plane?

The small seating area of the first class section on most planes offers a high probability for the nonsmoker in such sections to be thoroughly smoked up by smoking. It is a premium, executive privilege.

let's exercise today
instead of smoking away

quitting the habit

For the most part the degree of dependency and desire
to quit smoking has most to do with the probability of
success in stopping. Factors affecting the ability to quit
are:

- Self-realization of the dependency and the loss of
  freedom that smoking entails.

- The prospect of a smoke-free life and bid to escape
  the prospects of disability due to the habit.

- Understanding that relapse is a high probability
  and that success in stopping may depend on
  more than one effort to stop.

- The support of family and friends can be critical
  towards cessation.

- Family, friends, and employers need to realize that smoking is not just a "bad habit" but a serious dependency, psycho-active on the brain and nervous system, and an addiction more compelling than heroin.

A substantive reason for quitting is the cost to self and others. William L. Weiss, assistant professor of the Albers Graduate School of Business in Seattle, estimates that in addition to the personal cost for the tobacco product, attendant items, health-associated aggravations, maintenance, repair, and replacements, the employer loses about $4,000 per year in absenteeism, higher incidence of smokers' illness and death, loss in productivity, damage, maintenance, loss by burns and fire, and impact upon others.

Personal responsibility of the smoker to quit in deference to others, as well as self, is a growing issue. Such responsibility extends to family, friends, and other loved ones.

Another reinforcing attitude for the smoker in quitting is to feel anger at the purveyors of cigarettes, cigars, and pipes, and their manipulative campaigns to draw people into their addictive web and to strongly boycott their product and take an activist position against the tobacco industry. It would seem that a dedicated smoker, who is trying to quit, would have a large measure of anger that could be vented in such a constructive direction.

According to the American Cancer Society, about 95 percent of smokers quit "cold turkey." Some smokers, however, may want the assurance and support of professional help. Stop-smoking programs and classes are available from the American Cancer Society and the American Lung Association. Some hospitals, private clinics, churches, and other organizations also conduct smoking-cessation programs.

Smokers with a long-term habituation or heavy addiction are likely to need more consistent help than the light, short-term smoker. Each smoker is an individual with his or her own personal idiosyncrasies. The defenses and justifications upon which the smoker has consciously and subconsciously depended do not easily disperse into thin air. Personal introspection, persistent effort, encouragement from others, and a rebirth of attitudes are essential for the determination of most smokers to quit the habit. Stopping smoking should be viewed as a continuing process, not as an isolated event.

Those who have quit feel that they are born again and a burden has been lifted. The reward of a purer, freer life is the objective. Smokers should not be deterred if they fail to succeed in quitting the first time. Many persons have succeeded only after many tries.

An interesting thought in regard to quitting would be for our federal and/or state legislatures to outlaw nicotine or other addictive products present in cigarettes or other smoking materials. To compensate for those people who are addicted, physicians might be allowed to prescribe a moderating dosage of nicotine or other substances on a declining basis until the addicted person can handle a personal life with minimal or no such medicative support. In this manner large segments of the population could most likely be weaned away from the smoking habit.

In a recent move that approaches this suggestion, it was announced that the Food and Drug Administration is on the verge of approving the first prescription drug to help smokers quit the habit.[1] The product is called Nicorette, a chewing gum that contains nicotine. The gum is already being sold in Canada, Finland, Great Britain, Sweden, and Switzerland. Studies on the gum performed by a British doctor show that the success rate for quitting after one year is about 40 percent, much higher than other methods. One piece of the gum will contain the nicotine equivalent of one cigarette, which would be absorbed through the lining of the mouth.

---

[1] Sarah E. Moran, "Smokers to Get New Habit-Kicking Gum," *Denver Post,* Sept. 12, 1983.

Most smokers do not believe they are "hooked" on their habit; they believe they can quit smoking at any time. Facts do not align with this belief. There is increasing evidence that the number of cigarettes smoked per day is directly related to inability to quit smoking.[2]

Smokers who do quit achieve many immediate health benefits, the first being a rapid decline in the carbon monoxide level in the blood within 12 hours. Stamina and vigor improve and headaches and stomachaches caused by smoking disappear. Ex-smokers often notice a heightened sense of smell and taste.[3] Many ex-smokers experience feelings of improved health and well-being, but others may feel a variety of unpleasant, temporary side effects including irritability, anxiety, craving for tobacco, visual and sleep disturbances, and a distortion of time judgment. Generally all these physical effects subside within a week.[4]

health

Good health is difficult to exactly define. From the personal perspective, it is measured by feeling good. Many smokers feel good and do not exhibit any outward signs of harm from their habit. However, the larger view of smoking is fraught with the dark shadows of chronic impairment and lethal diseases.

The annals of disease tied to chemical, statistical, demographic, and scientific observation and evaluation overwhelmingly indict the inhalation of ignited tobacco as a cause of minor and major maladies and in hastening the termination of life. Inasmuch as smoking is a compulsion only of the addicted, and smoking is dangerous to health, it seems reasonable that our societal efforts should be vigorously increased towards creating ex-smokers.

---

[2] American Cancer Society, *Dangers of Smoking — Benefits of Quitting & Relative Risks of Reduced Exposure,* rev. ed. (New York: American Cancer Society, Inc., 1980). p. 60.

[3] Ibid., p. 7.   [4] Ibid., p. 57.

By any means, all nonsmokers do not enjoy pristine health. The stressful racking of the human mind and body by the extremes in violence, noise, misapplied chemistry, nuclear might, political unrest, and economic displacement takes its toll. Our national state of health has slipped. Smoking remains a massive national problem despite the fact that ex-smokers are increasing in number. Smoking remains a critical stress upon all other stresses.

We all know the route to better health: Stop smoking; adopt aerobic forms of exercise; eat natural unprocessed foods; cut back on saturated fats, sugar, alcohol, salt, and caffeine; drink pure water; and avoid excessive stress. If you are not allergic to them, get a dog, cat, or canary. Avoid radioactivity and all forms of pollutants. The ever-growing health consciousness of the American public is illustrated by a Gallup Poll taken in 1979 in which 65 percent of the people wanted natural foods. Tobacco is a natural product but remains innocuous until it is burned, chewed, or snuffed.

Smoking is psychoaddictive. It consumes the personality of the heavily addicted smoker. Its inner cravings are hard to stem, but the more that a smoker indulges in the mounting vigor of aerobics, avoids alcohol, avoids strong spices and seasonings, avoids caffeine or other drug-like substances, shuns other smokers, and substitutes physical action for idleness, the greater the chance that the smoker can succeed in terminating the habit instead of the smoker.

science and medicine

Since around 1960, intensive scientific and medical studies have been made of the effects of tobacco smoking upon the smoker. More recently, studies have included the effect of smoking upon the health of the nonsmoker. The Surgeon Generals' reports embodying a host of individual studies plus other scientific, medical, and technical papers attest to the serious harm and death attributable to cigarette, cigar, and pipe smoking. In addition to fearsome cancer and heart disease, a retinue of other minor and major maladies are associated with smoking.

In the present 1983 annual report, Surgeon General C. Everett Koop states, **"The excess mortality experienced by cigarette smokers is beyond challenge"** and one out of 10 Americans will *prematurely die of smoking-related heart disease.* Koop further said heart disease increases with the number of cigarettes smoked, total years of smoking, and degree of inhalation. Women who smoke and use birth control pills run a 10 times greater risk of heart disease than nonsmoking women not on the pill.

Heart disease, the leading cause of death in the United States, kills about 565,000 Americans annually with 170,000 deaths attributed to smoking. Cigarette smoking results in 129,000 cancer deaths a year. Smokers of over two packs a day have a heart disease death rate nearly 200 percent greater than nonsmokers.

Koop noted that smokers **"can and do reduce their risk of coronary heart disease and earlier death when they quit smoking."** 55 million Americans smoke over 30 cigarettes a day *"...an incredible assault upon the health of Americans ... which we must reduce."*

(Emphasis added)

each cigarette is one too many

harm from smoking

The effects of cigarette smoking on health have been presented to the United States public since the 1950s. Each year, more and more evidence on the harmful effects of smoking is gathered, and new research findings are constantly emerging. Unfortunately, news reports in the press or on radio and television usually only briefly highlight the findings this information reports. Examining copies of the reports in detail provides a more comprehensive and sobering view of smoking as "the chief, single, avoidable cause of death in our society and *the most important public health issue of our time.*"[1]

This section of the book examines the dimensions of harm caused by cigarette smoking, not only to one's health if a smoker, but also to nonsmokers and the indoor environ-

---

[1] United States, Department of Health and Human Services, Public Health Service, Off. on Smoking and Health, *The Health Consequences of Smoking: Cancer* (Washington, D.C.: U.S. Govt. Printing Off., 1982), p. xi, emphasis added.

ment. The data on the effects of smoking on health and the chemical components of cigarette smoke were obtained from the 1981 and 1982 Surgeon General's reports.

heart disease

In the 1981 report, Surgeon General Julius Richmond writes "... it is important to recognize that the largest component of excess mortality caused by smoking is cardiovascular disease deaths."[2] Cigarette smoking and coronary heart disease are dose-related: As the number of cigarettes smoked increases, the incidence of coronary heart disease increases. Stopping smoking results in a decrease in the incidence of coronary heart disease. Cigarette smoking interacts synergistically with other heart-disease risk factors, such as hypertension and hypercholesterolemia, to multiply risk.

Nicotine in cigarette smoke elevates blood pressure and heart rate and causes constriction of cutaneous (skin) blood vessels, all of which usually result in making the heart work harder. Smoking is also associated with atherosclerosis, which may also contribute to increased cardiovascular disease.

Carbon monoxide in cigarette smoke places a burden on the circulatory system because of its great affinity for hemoglobin in the blood, approximately 210 times greater than that of oxygen. It combines with hemoglobin to form carboxyhemoglobin. Carbon monoxide reduces the oxygen-carrying capacity of the blood.

cancer

"Cigarette smoking is the major single cause of cancer mortality in the United States."[3] Smokers have total

[2] United States, Department of Health and Human Services, Public Health Service, Off. on Smoking and Health, *The Health Consequences of Smoking: The Changing Cigarette* (Washington, D.C.: U.S. Govt. Printing Off., 1981), p. vi.
[3] *The Health Consequences of Smoking: Cancer,* p. v.

cancer-death rates two times greater than nonsmokers. For heavy smokers (more than one pack per day) the excess risk of cancer mortality is three to four times greater compared with nonsmokers. The overall cancer-mortality rates for smokers are dose-related as measured by the daily amount of cigarettes smoked. Quitting smoking, especially cigarettes, is the most effective action a person can take to reduce cancer risk.

Lung cancer contributes most to the overall cancer-death rate (25 percent). An estimated 85 percent of lung-cancer cases are caused by cigarette smoking. Lung cancer is a very fatal disease: The five-year survival rate of less than 10 percent has not changed in twenty years.

In addition to lung cancer, cigarette smoking is a major cause of cancers in the larynx, oral cavity, and esophagus. It is a contributory factor in the development of cancers of the bladder, pancreas, and kidney and a probable link to stomach cancer. A recent study (reported in the *Journal of the American Medical Association*) confirms a significant relationship between cigarette smoking and cervical cancer.* Smokers were found to be at an increased risk of dysplasia and carcinoma of the cervix, and the risk increased with increased cumulative exposure to cigarettes. The risk of smokers was greatest in those who started smoking as teenagers.

chronic obstruction lung disease (cold)

The relationship between cigarette smoking and chronic obstructive lung disease (chronic bronchitis and emphysema) is well known. 95 to 98 percent of all emphysema is cigarette-smoke related. The development of airway obstruction is closely related to the amount of cigarettes smoked. There is biochemical evidence that cigarette smoke paralyzes the lung's defenses against injury,

*"Cervical Cancer Linked to Cigarette Smoking," *Let's Live*, vol. 51, no. 11, p. 6.

according to Dr. Robert Sandhaus, senior staff physician at the National Jewish Hospital/National Asthma Center. Smokers of low-tar and low-nicotine brands who compensate by deeper inhalation or more smoking could be increasing their risk of developing COLD. A person's smoking pattern is very important in determining the relative amount of smoke constituents that reach the lungs and the subsequent airway response to inhaled smoke. Holding the smoke in the mouth before inhaling produces less airway response than direct inhalation.

smoking and pregnancy

Cigarette smoking during pregnancy has adverse effects on the mother, the fetus, the placenta, the newborn infant, and the child in later years. Pregnant women who smoke increase the risk of spontaneous abortion, premature delivery, fetal death, and perinatal death (near the time of birth). The fetuses of smoking mothers have higher blood carboxyhemoglobin levels and lower arterial oxygen levels than do the mothers. Many studies have consistently shown that maternal smoking has an adverse effect on newborn-infant birth weight, reducing birth weight an average of 200 grams (seven ounces).

A recent study concerning children of smoking mothers found that the rate of lung growth of the children was lower than normal, and that the youngsters may face an increased risk of chronic obstructive lung disease later in life.[3A]

The five-year study looked at 1,156 children, aged 5 to 9, who lived in east Boston, and the results were published in the *New England Journal of Medicine*. The study reported that the lungs of nonsmoking children whose mothers smoked grew at a rate 7 percent less than those whose mothers did not smoke. "These data suggest that maternal smoking contributes to a reduction in the rate

---

[3A] "Mothers' Smoking Linked to Children's Slower Lung Growth." Associated Press wire story. *Boulder Daily Camera*, Sept. 22, 1983. p. 3A.

of development of lung function in children and, along with the child's own smoking habits, may be important in the development of chronic obstructive disease of the airways in adult life," the researchers wrote. The doctors were not certain whether the slow lung growth was caused by smoking during pregnancy or by breathing smoke-filled air at home.

Other studies suggest that older children (up to 11 years) of smoking mothers have slight but measurable deficits in physical growth, emotional development, intellectual ability, and behavior.

chemical components of tobacco smoke

Tobacco smoke is a very complex and diverse mixture of components. Over 3,600 different chemical substances have been identified in cigarette smoke, including many suspected or proven toxic agents, carcinogens, cocarcinogens, and tumor initiators. The composition of tobacco smoke is a function of the chemical and physical properties of the leaf or tobacco blend, the wrapper, the filler, and the way the tobacco is burned. The burning core of a cigarette can reach temperatures up to 950 degrees Celsius (1742 degrees Fahrenheit).

The major toxic agents in cigarette smoke are listed in the tables that follow:

TABLE 1.—Major toxic agents in the gas phase of cigarette smoke (unaged)*

Agent	Biologic activity[a]	Concentration/cigarette		
		Range reported		U.S. cigarettes[b]
Dimethylnitrosamine	C	1—200	ng	13	ng
Ethylmethylnitrosamine	C	0.1—10	ng	1.8	ng
Diethylnitrosamine	C	0—10	ng	1.5	ng
Nitrosopyrrolidine	C	2—42	ng	11	ng
Other nitrosamines (4 compounds)	C	0—20	ng	?	
Hydrazine	C	24—43	ng	32	ng
Vinyl chloride	C	1—16	ng	12	ng
Urethane	TI	10—35	ng	30	ng
Formaldehyde	CT, CoC	20—90	μg	30	μg
Hydrogen cyanide	CT, T	30—200	μg	110	μg
Acrolein	CT	25—140	μg	70	μg
Acetaldehyde	CT	18—1,400	μg	800	μg
Nitrogen oxides (NO_x)[c]	T	10—600	μg	350	μg
Ammonia	T?[d]	10—150	μg	60	μg
Pyridine	T?[d]	9—93	μg	10	μg
Carbon monoxide	T	2—20	mg	17	mg

*Cigarettes may also contain such carcinogens as arsine, nickel carbonyl, and possibly volatile chlorinated olefins and nitro-olefins.

[a]C denotes carcinogen; TI, tumor initiator; CoC, cocarcinogen; CT, cilia toxic agent; and T, toxic agent.

[b]85 mm cigarettes without filter tips bought on the open market 1973-1976.

[c]NO_x >95% NO; rest NO_2.

[d]Not toxic in smoke of blended U.S. cigarettes because pH <6.5, and therefore ammonia and pyridines are present only in protonated form.

SOURCE: Wynder and Hoffman (190).

TABLE 2.—Major toxic agents in the particulate matter of cigarette smoke (unaged)*

Agent	Biologic activity[a]	Concentration/cigarette			
		Range reported		U.S. cigarettes[b]	
Benzo[a]pyrene	TI	8–50	ng	20	ng
5-Methylchrysene	TI	0.5–2	ng	0.6	ng
Benzo[j]fluoranthene	TI	5–40	ng	10	ng
Benz[a]anthracene	TI	5–80	ng	40	ng
Other polynuclear aromatic hydrocarbons (>20 compounds)	TI	?		?	
Dibenz[a,j]acridine	TI	3–10	ng	8	ng
Dibenz[a,h]acridine	TI	?		?	
Dibenzo[c,g]carbazole	TI	0.7	ng	0.7	ng
Pyrene	CoC	50–200	ng	150	ng
Fluoranthene	CoC	50–250	ng	170	ng
Benzo[g,h,i]perylene	CoC	10–60	ng	30	ng
Other polynuclear aromatic hydrocarbons (>10 compounds)	CoC	?		?	
Naphthalenes	CoC	1–10	μg	6	μg
1-Methylindoles	CoC	0.3–0.9	μg	0.8	μg
9-Methylcarbazoles	CoC	0.005–0.2	μg	0.1	μg
Other neutral compounds	CoC	?		?	
Catechol	CoC	40–460	μg	270	μg
3- & 4-Methylcatechols	CoC	30–40	μg	32	μg
Other catechols (>4 compounds)	CoC	?		?	
Unknown phenols and acids	CoC	?		?	
N'-Nitrosonornicotine	C	100–250	ng	250	ng
Other nonvolatile nitrosamines	C	?		?	
β-Naphthylamine	BC	0–25	ng	20	ng
Other aromatic amines	BC	?		?	
Unknown nitro compounds	BC	?		?	
Polonium-210	C	0.03–1.3	pCi	?	
Nickel compounds	C	10–600	ng	?	
Cadmium compounds	C	09–70	ng	?	
Arsenic	C	1–25	μg	?	
Nicotine	T	0.1–2.0	mg	1.5	mg
Minor tobacco alkaloids	T	0.01–0.2	mg	0.1	mg
Phenol	CT	10–200	μg	85	μg
Cresols (3 compounds)	CT	10–150	μg	70	μg

*Incomplete list.
[a]C denotes carcinogen; BC, bladder carcinogen; CoC, cocarcinogen; TI, tumor initiator; CT, cilia toxic agent; and T, toxic agent.
[b]85 mm cigarettes without filter tips bought on the open market 1973-1976.
SOURCE: Wynder and Hoffman *(190)*.

SOURCE: *The Health Consequences of Smoking: The Changing Cigarette,* p. 34.

additives

Flavorings and chemical additives are being added to low-tar and low-nicotine cigarettes to increase consumer acceptance. Tests on flavor additives produced traces of mutagenic compounds. Cigarette manufacturers are not required to reveal what additives are being used, so no assessment of their risk can be made. At the present time, no federal agency in the United States oversees or regulates cigarette manufacturing.

nicotine

Nicotine appears to be the most important acute-acting pharmocologic agent in tobacco smoke and the primary pharmacologic reinforcer. Besides the physiological effects noted earlier (elevated blood pressure, peripheral vasoconstriction), nicotine can also permit the formation of tobacco-specific nitrosamines, which are potent carcinogens. Nicotine itself may be a significant cocarcinogen. Nicotine also has been found to have potent physiological effects on the gastrointestinal, endocrine, and central-nervous systems. When inhaled, nicotine is rapidly absorbed by the lungs and enters the bloodstream quickly, reaching the brain in less than eight seconds.

Nicotine is a very potent poison. The amount of nicotine in a single cigarette is sufficient to kill a small child, according to Dr. Robert Sandhaus of the National Jewish Hospital. Fortunately, these types of deaths are virtually unknown because swallowing tobacco induces severe vomiting, reducing the dose of nicotine that enters the bloodstream.

Cigarette smokers absorb nicotine through inhalation more quickly than pipe or cigar smokers or persons using chewing tobacco or snuff. Nicotine acts on specialized receptors in the brain that recognize and react to its presence in the body. Nicotine affects the body in different ways: It can act as a tranquilizer in stressful situations while, during calm times, it can act as a stimulant similar to amphetamines. Nicotine appears to be a physiologically addictive drug, similar to opium derivatives, that is psychoactive (affecting the chemistry of the brain and central nervous system), creates dependence, and leads to compulsive use.

A smoker with a pack-a-day habit takes more than 70,000 puffs a year, a frequency of "hits" unmatched by any other drug taking. Thus, the habit is tremendously "overlearned," and it is not easy to stop such rewarding behavior.[3B]

side-stream smoke

Increasing concern is being raised about the probable hazardous effects of inhaling side-stream smoke; that is, smoke given off by the smouldering cigarette into the ambient air. Side-stream and mainstream smoke contain similar chemical constituents, including known carcinogens, some of which are present in much higher concentrations in side-stream smoke. The table below gives toxic and tumorigenic components in cigarette smoke and the ratio of these compounds in side-stream to mainstream smoke.

[3B]American Cancer Society, *Dangers of Smoking — Benefits of Quitting & Relative Risks of Reduced Exposure,* rev. ed. (New York: American Cancer Society, Inc., 1980), p. 55.

TABLE 10.—Toxic and tumorigenic agents of cigarette smoke; ratio of sidestream smoke (SS) to mainstream smoke (MS)

A. Gas phase	Amount/cigarette		SS/MS
Carbon dioxide	10 - 80	mg	8.1[1]
Carbon monoxide	0.5 - 26	mg	2.5[1]
Nitrogen oxides (NO_x)	16 - 600	μg	4.7 - 5.8
Ammonia	10 - 130	μg	44 - 73
Hydrogen cyanide	280 - 550	μg	0.17 - 0.37
Hydrazine	32	μg	3
Formaldehyde	20 - 90	μg	51
Acetone	100 - 940	μg	2.5 - 3.2
Acrolein	10 - 140	μg	12
Acetonitrile	60 - 160	μg	10
Pyridine	32	μg	10
3-Vinylpyridine	23	μg	28
N-Nitrosodimethylamine	4 - 180	ng	10 - 830
N-Nitrosoethylmethylamine	1.0 - 40	ng	5 - 12
N-Nitrosodiethylamine	0.1 - 28	ng	4 - 25
N-Nitrosopyrrolidine	0 - 110	ng	3 - 76

B. Particulate phase	Amount/cigarette		SS/MS
Total particulate phase	0.1 - 40	mg	1.3 - 1.9[1]
Nicotine	0.06 - 2.3	mg	2.6 - 3.3[1]
Toluene	108	μg	5.6
Phenol	20 - 150	μg	2.6
Catechol	40 - 280	μg	0.7
Stigmasterol	53	μg	0.8
Total phytosterols	130	μg	0.8
Naphthalene	2.8	μg	16
1-Methylnaphthalene	1.2	μg	26
2-Methylnaphthalene	1.0	μg	29
Phenanthrene	2.0 - 80	ng	2.1
Benz(a)anthracene	10 - 70	ng	2.7
Pyrene	15 - 90	ng	1.9 - 3.6
Benzo(a)pyrene	8 - 40	ng	2.7 - 3.4
Quinoline	1.7	μg	11
Methylquinoline	6.7	μg	11
Harmane	1.1 - 3.1	μg	0.7 - 2.7
Norharmane	3.2 - 8.1	μg	1.4 - 4.3
Aniline	100 - 1,200	ng	30
o-Toluidine	32	ng	19
1-Naphthylamine	1.0 - 22	ng	39
2-Napthylamine	4.3 - 27	ng	39
4-Aminobiphenyl	2.4 - 4.6	ng	31
N'-Nitrosonornicotine	0.2 - 3.7	μg	1 - 5
NNK[2]	0.12 - 0.44	μg	1 - 8
N'-Nitrosoanatabine	0.15 - 4.6	μg	1 - 7
N-Nitrosodiethanolamine	0 - 40	ng	1.2

[1]In cigarettes with perforated filter tips the SS/MS ratio rises with increasing air dilution. In the case of smoke dilution with air to 17 percent, the SS/MS ratios for TPM rise to 2.14, CO_2 36.5, CO 23.5, and nicotine to 13.1.

[2]NNK = 4-(Methylnitrosamino)-1-(3-pyridyl)-1-butanone.

SOURCE: Hoffman et al. (82).

SOURCE: *The Health Consequences of Smoking: Cancer*, p. 214.

The Surgeon General has written:

"... involuntary smoking may pose a carcinogenic risk to the nonsmoker. Any health risk resulting from involuntary smoke exposure is a serious public-health concern because of the large numbers of nonsmokers in the population who are potentially exposed. Therefore, for the purpose of preventive medicine, prudence dictates that nonsmokers avoid exposure to secondhand tobacco smoke to the extent possible."[4]

other effects of smoking

Smoking puts extra biologic demands on the human body; for example, smoking depletes levels of vitamin C in the blood. One study showed that smoking one cigarette neutralizes in the body about 25 milligrams of vitamin C.[5] A heavy smoker will be deficient in vitamin C unless supplements are taken.

The ingestion of carotene and vitamin A and other means of disease-preventative nutrition may reduce the harm of smoking. Smoking tends to constrict the blood vessels and impair the heart. Vitamin E and lecithin tend to open the blood vessels and remove arterial plaques.

Another finding concerning the effects of smoking is that smoking suppresses the natural endorphin (pain-relieving) production of the brain. Endorphins are morphine-like, natural pain inhibitors. Some pain clinics will not accept smokers because of this endorphin-suppression factor. Thus compared to nonsmokers, smokers may be expected to experience greater pain.

---

[4] *The Health Consequences of Smoking: Cancer,* p. viii.
[5] Irwin Stone, *The Healing Factor: "Vitamin C" Against Disease* (New York: Grosset and Dunlap, 1972), p. 174.

taste and smell

For the most part, smokers suffer from a loss of taste and smell. Because of this loss, they are generally unaware of the unpleasant, odoriferous, and stenchful aspects of their habit. In the matter of taste, they miss many of the subtle delights of sensitively prepared food.

New studies reveal that taste is largely dependent upon the response of olifactory sensors located at the upper region of the nasal cavity. Food odors reach the nasal receptors by moving behind the palate. Olifactory lobes attached to the brain are connected to the nervous receptors. Various areas of the brain receive stimulations in cognition, emotion, and deep-seated memory. The nose is designed to produce air turbulence over its inner bone structure, which enhances the perception of smell. The olifactory neurons are the only nerve cells of our body that regenerate every 30 to 60 days. There are approximately five million neurons—specialized nasal-receptor cells—in each nasal cavity. Very young children, elderly persons, and smokers have less perception of either pleasant aromas or unpleasant odors and less discriminating taste in food and drink.

The American Lung Association, in its brochure, "Second-Hand Smoke" (Am. Lung Assn., 1982), p. 7., has the following comment:

> "Another intriguing finding from air-conditioning research is that the human body attracts tobacco smoke. Burning tobacco smoke creates a high electrical potential, whereas the water-filled human body has a low one. The smoke in a room gravitates and clings to people in much the same way as iron filings are drawn to a magnet.
>
> "And the odors linger on. Chemicals in tobacco smoke called aldehydes and ketones supply the penetrating smell, while the tars hold them to your

skin and your clothes. But the smoker is not sensitive to the smell because of the destructive effects of smoke on the inner lining of his or her nose."

lower-tar and lower-nicotine cigarettes: a safer cigarette?

Many smokers have switched to low-tar and low-nicotine brands to reduce the health risks of smoking; however, this strategy may have some serious drawbacks. The advertised measurements of tar and nicotine content determined by smoking machines may not reflect the actual dosage the smoker receives, because the machines are limited in accurately reproducing human smoking behavior. Smokers often take more-frequent, larger, higher-velocity puffs. These compensatory adjustments can actually turn low-tar and low-nicotine cigarettes into higher-tar and higher-nicotine versions. Smokers also compensate for reduced nicotine levels in low-nicotine brands by smoking more cigarettes.

Some lower-yield cigarettes use ventilation holes in the filters to dilute the smoke with air, reducing the amounts of tar, nicotine, and carbon monoxide in each puff. Some smokers block the ventilation holes with their lips, fingers, or even tape, thereby—unwittingly or purposely—defeating the purpose of the holes. If these holes are blocked, yields to the smoker of nicotine, tar, and carbon monoxide can increase by about two, three, and four times, respectively. And as mentioned earlier, the addition of various additives and flavorings poses additional, unknown risks. Because of compensatory smoking and the possible hazards of additives, smokers who switch to lower-tar and lower-nicotine cigarettes are likely to inhale as many harmful compounds as smokers of regular, higher-tar and nicotine brands.

A new study by researchers at San Francisco General Hospital Medical Center (reported in the July 21, 1983 *New England Journal of Medicine*) found that cigarette advertising claims and Federal Trade Commission data systematically understated smokers' exposure to nicotine in cigarettes. Essentially, low-yield cigarette smokers consume as much of the addictive and toxic substances in tobacco as do regular-cigarette smokers. The researchers found that the health benefits of switching to low-yield (low-tar and low-nicotine) cigarettes are insignificant and may be nonexistant, and that claims made about low-yield cigarettes give smokers a false sense of security. The study also found that tobacco from "light" cigarette brands contained more nicotine by weight than most regular cigarettes.

harm to the indoor environment

Smoking damages other things besides people. The fire danger is probably the greatest harm: 56 percent of all fatal residential fires are caused by careless smokers.[6] Increased maintenance, damage to furniture and furnishings, objectionable odors, contamination of duct systems, deleterious effects on laboratory and computer equipment, and other consequences of smoking add to the dimensions of harm. These aspects of smoking as well as its direct and indirect economic impacts, are discussed later in the book.

additional harmful effects from smoking

osteoporosis

Cigarette smoking has been demonstrated to induce bone demineralization leading to osteoporosis. Acidity of the bone structure is caused by smoking that results in the increased demineralization.[7]

---

[6] William Weiss, "Smoking: Burning a Hole in the Balance Sheet," *Personnel Management,* vol. 13, no. 5, May 1981, p. 25.

[7] Charles Gerras, ed., *The Encyclopedia of Common Diseases* (Emmaus, PA: Rodale Press, 1976), p. 277.

colds

Smokers tend to get more severe and frequent colds and have a more difficult time getting over them.[8] Each cigarette smoked paralyzes the cilia (microscopic hairs) of the respiratory passages for 30 to 40 minutes. The normal sweeping action of the cilia is thereby impaired in protecting the body from invading, harmful microorganisms. Smokers lose this valuable defense against infection.

ulcers

Cigarette smoking has been associated with ulcer formation. Buffering secretions from the pancreas and bile that normally protect the duodenum are inhibited by the inhalation of nicotine. Output of gastric juices is increased, increasing probabilities of ulceration.[9]

cadmium

Cigarettes are a major source of cadmium (a toxic metal) in the human body that has been linked with emphysema.[10]

new findings

Dr. Edward A. Martell of the National Center for Atmospheric Research (NCAR) has determined that radon present in homes and buildings is critical in inducing lung cancer and other diseases under conditions of indoor smoking. Natural radon gas is transported from soils through wet and porous structural material, building materials, and well water. Radon-decay products become at-

---

[8] Ibid., pp. 409, 410.

[9] Ibid, p. 1231.

[10] Ibid., p. 625.

tached to airborne smoke particles and are deposited in the bronchi, producing radioactive (alpha-radiation) hot spots. As bronchial-tissue injury progresses, lead-210-enriched smoke particles persist in damaged tissue. Thereafter, polonium-210 (decay product of lead-210) substantially elevates the alpha radiation dose.

Martell says, "It is very likely that most nonsmokers who acquire lung cancer are passive smokers." (Passive smokers are nonsmokers who breathe the smokers' smoke).

Lung cancer is the leading cause of cancer death in men. It is the second leading cause of cancer death in women, but, as increasing numbers of women smoke, it is expected to equal that of men by 1985.

Another, newly released study also related to radioactive elements was recently issued by the Environmental Protection Agency.[1] The eight-year study determined levels of plutonium in the lungs and livers of eastern Colorado residents who live near the Rocky Flats nuclear-weapons plant (which is located 16 miles northwest of Denver). The findings indicate that only smokers have above-average plutonium levels, "apparently because their lungs were damaged and couldn't cleanse themselves efficiently."[2]

---

[1] Todd Malmsbury, "Eight-Year Flats Study Says Plutonium Levels Normal," *Boulder Daily Camera,* May 13, 1983.

[2] Ibid.

radon, odors, and smoking

Hair and hair-like textures, such as carpet, drapes, upholstery, and clothing, retain odoriferous and contaminating residues from the smoking of tobacco. Hair and similar natural and synthetic fibers have an affinity for airborne radon-decay products present in the indoor atmosphere.[1] Radon gas originates from the radioactive decay of radium-226 in soils and, in some cases, in structural materials. Radon is liberated as a gas under conditions of reduced atmospheric pressure or by transport in solution in the presence of high soil-moisture conditions.

Cigarette and other tobacco-smoke particles are deposited electrostatically on the tips of hairs and hair-like surfaces. The odoriferous particulates accumulate the radon-decay products present in the air. Paper and documents can be included as having hairy surfaces as well as the fine hairs that cover exposed skin surfaces of man and animal.

An indication of the degree of localized, indoor, smoke contamination can be readily detected by nonsmokers with a normal sense of smell. Unwrap any drawings or papers that have been exposed to cigarette smoke and an individual with a sensitive nose may be able to determine the intensity and even the type of tobacco smoke that was burned. The odor- and radon-progeny-bearing particles of tobacco smoke present not only an immediate threat to well-being, composure, possessions, and interior space but also a serious, delayed risk of lung cancer and other chronic health effects. Aerosols commonly used to freshen indoor air mask or compound the problem and serve no useful purpose.

---

[1] Based on experimental observations by or personal communication from Dr. Edward A. Martell, National Center for Atmospheric Research, Boulder, Colorado.

more findings

smoke gets in your eyes

Another, lesser publicized effect of tobacco smoke is the potential danger of serious damage to the eyes and a lessening of total visual ability. Researchers have now found strong correlations between proximity of smoke and optical damage to both smokers and nonsmokers.[1] Specifically, smoking can affect vision in the following ways:[2]

- Reduction of night vision — nicotine and carbon monoxide combine to restrict blood vessels and oxygen supply to the eye, which can interfere with adaptation to light in a dark environment.

- Narrowing of the field of view — smoking tends to narrow the field of view, with the result that the reduced image seen by the eye and sent to the brain can impair peripheral vision.

- Tobacco amblyopia — dietary deficiencies, alcohol abuse, and smoking can create amblyopia, a dimness of sight characterized by loss of visual sharpness and degrees of color blindness, and in some cases, total blindness.

- Eye irritation — the 1972 Surgeon General's report documented eye irritation in nonsmokers and found that about 70 percent of the eye irritation complaints derived from tobacco smoke, regardless of whether the sufferer was allergic or nonallergic. Contact lens wearers are particularly susceptible to smoke irritation.

---

[1] John O'Rouke, "Smoke Eyes," *Let's Live,* vol. 51, no. 6, pp. 55-59.
[2] Ibid.

With the prevalence of indoor smoking in our society, it becomes apparent that smoke gets in *everyones'* eyes. Opthamologists note that the eye and surrounding structures are very delicate and easily damaged. Avoidance of tobacco smoke whenever possible to prevent possible eye damage is particularly advisable.

smoking linked to ear infection

A group of doctors from Seattle's Children's Orthopedic Hospital and Medical Center, writing in the *Journal of the American Medical Association*, have stated that breathing cigarette smoke can contribute to the development of chronic, middle-ear disease in children.[3] Exposure to smoking in the home appeared to be the single, most important item related to the majority of all children with the chronic ear infections. The report stated, "Exposure to one or more household cigarette smokers increased the risk for persistent middle-ear effusions nearly three-fold. With household exposure to smoke from more than three packs of cigarettes a day, the risk increased four-fold."[4]

damage to hearing

In a booklet published by the American Cancer Society, *World Smoking and Health*, a study performed by two Egyptian doctors at the Cairo University Hospital Clinic found that smoking increases the incidence and severity of deafness.[5] The doctors stated that smoking encourages the development of atherosclerosis (hardening of the arteries), which could impair the brain's blood supply and cause a functional deficiency that might affect hearing.

---

[3] "Ear Infection Linked to Cigarette Smoking," *Better Nutrition,* vol. 43, no. 6, p. 6.
[4] Ibid.
[5] "Smoking and Deafness," Nutrition in the News, *Better Nutrition,* vol. 42, no. 12, p. 6.

Of 150 smokers, 70 percent had some degree of deafness, compared 16.6 percent of 150 nonsmokers. Both groups were men aged 20 to 50. For each smoker the average hearing loss was 25.3 percent; for each nonsmoker hearing loss averaged 8.8 percent.[6]

The study found that damage to hearing caused by chronic smoking was greater than that caused by aging.

smoking and religion

Most religions seek a state of purity for the human condition. In the Bible for example, we can find statements such as, "... Every other sin which a man commits is outside the body; but the immoral man sins against his own body. Do you not know that your body is a temple of the Holy Spirit within you, which you have from God? ... So glorify God in your body."[1] It seems that anyone feeling truly religious about the spirit and magnificence of the body would not smoke. Smoking is forbidden or discouraged by some religions. The Amish, members of the Church of Jesus Christ of Latter-Day Saints (Mormons), and Seventh-Day Adventists are cases in point.

The Amish is the most isolated nonsmoking society. Thus, lung cancer occurs only rarely among the Amish— as rarely, it seems, as the Amish smoke. A few Amish men smoke cigars, some chew tobacco, and some Amish youngsters have started to smoke cigarettes.

> "Mortality ratios from all respiratory diseases were significantly lower by over 80 percent in Amish males 40-60 years old and by 50 percent in those 70 or older ... In the chronic pulmonary disease category, including emphysema, bronchitis, and asthma, only one Amish death occurred with approximately twenty-three expected deaths. This lower number of

---

[6] Ibid.
[1] 1 Cor. 6:18-20.

deaths was highly significant and may reflect the relative absence of cigarettes and urban and occupational air pollution."[2]

It is sometimes argued that relaxed, rural living, and not the absence of cigarette smoking causes less respiratory disease among the Amish. Although diet, breeding habits, and life-style do affect results, there is no reason to conclude that the Amish experience less stress, and there may be reason to conclude that they experience more as they reject the surrounding society.[3] As for urban air pollutants, they "probably contribute less than 5 percent of the cases of lung cancer in the United States."[4] Urban and occupational air pollutants, however, have a greater impact on smokers, possibly because of interaction with smoking.

Mormons in the Utah Cancer Society have much lower— and "active" or particularly religious Mormons have even lower—lung-cancer mortality rates than non-Mormons.[5] In California, the number of lung-cancer deaths among Seventh-Day Adventists is only 20 percent that of the non-Seventh-Day Adventists.[6]

[2] R.F. Hamman, J.I. Barancik, A.M. Lilienfeld, "Patterns of Mortality in the Old Order of Amish: Background and Major Causes of Death," *American Journal of Epidemiology,* vol. 114, no. 6, Dec. 1981, p. 856.
[3] Ibid., p. 846.
[4] United States, Dept. of Health and Human Services, Public Health Serv., Off. of Smoking and Health, *The Health Consequences of Smoking: Cancer* (Washington, D.C., U.S. Govt. Printing Off., 1982), pp. 46-47.
[5] Ibid., p. 48.
[6] Ibid., p. 50.

unsmoked air is beautiful

pure, breathable air

It is a pleasure to breathe pure air. It is a difficult commodity to get in our polluted outdoor atmosphere and indoor atmosphere more intensely polluted with tobacco smoke. Smokers as well as nonsmokers are likely to enjoy the brief interludes when a breath of fresh air comes by.

Our atmosphere contains 21 percent oxygen that supports our metabolic systems. The effectiveness of our breathing depends upon what else the air contains besides oxygen.

The indoor atmosphere can be highly polluted within confined spaces where even moderate amounts of smoking prevail. Chain-smokers can produce an inexorable density of smoke that usurps the breathable air. If we could but directly tax smokers to the degree that they pollute the air, perhaps their level of consciousness would at least be elevated to their insult to our indoor atmosphere.

Side-stream smoke from an idling cigarette can produce 1.3 to 1.9 times the amount of airborne particulates, compared to the amount in the mainstream smoke that the smoker inhales. This contamination of the indoor atmosphere precludes the joy of breathing clean air. At best, other atmospheric outdoor and indoor pollutants do not cause a greater burden or a probable synergistic, deleterious effect upon health and vitality than the unnecessary addition of tobacco effluents.

In a recent issue of the *ASH Smoking and Health Review*, it was reported that a cigarette company had advertised for a chemist to work on the room odor of side-stream smoke.[1] This suggests that the tobacco company may be attempting to mask the standard cigarette stench with some type of additive. Disguising the smell of side-stream smoke with a more pleasant aroma in no way lessens its harm to those passively inhaling the fumes.

profile of a smoker

Some of the nicest, kindest, and most considerate people in the world are smokers; however, their ennobling assets seldom extend to their smoking. In the real world, they are responding to the tolerance of our society. It is a society that grew up with smoking in private and public places. In this setting, most smokers do not see themselves as uncaring and destructive persons. The intensively harmful and contaminating nature of cigarettes, cigars, and pipes has not been a primary concern of most smokers or nonsmokers.

Oral, visual, and manipulative gratifications are strong elements of addiction. Smoking, puffing, feeling, and seeing the issue of smoke and the handling and caressing of the addictive instrument (a cigarette, cigar, or pipe) reinforces habituation. Smokers who try to quit (and most do)

---

[1] Action on Smoking and Health, *Smoking and Health Review*, vol. 13, no. 5. (Washington, D.C.: ASH, 1983), p. 6.

find these repetitive habits most problematic to their desire to quit. Smokers who run out of cigarettes can find themselves mimicking this sensory habituation while craving a nicotine and chemical fix.

Smoking becomes a form of body language that tends to set an example for others in either a role model or peer group. Parents provide a smoking role for their children; celebrities provide smoking roles for those who identify with them; and peer groups provide a smoking role for those at any age who identify with the group.

This is particularly evident among teenagers. Penelope Eckert of the University of Michigan Anthropology Department supports the deglamorization and ridicule of smoking gestures, without putting the smoker down, as more effective in defusing the person from the smoking habit. On the high-school scene, she has observed that symbolic, smoking gestures, such as greeting and exchanging cigarettes, serve as a social bond. College candidates are not apt to smoke so openly as those who resent school or are more oriented to working-class attitudes. Eckert states that the symbology defines the students as "jocks" ("preppies," "frats," "collegiates," or "socialites") who don't favor smoking or "burnouts" ("hoods," "greasers," "stoners," or "freaks") who do. The status division of smokers and nonsmokers apparently is more definitive in larger schools.[1]

This information coincides with the tendency of smoking to be much less prevalent among executives than among workers. Unfortunately, girls and women have fallen heir to the devastations of smoking to their health and personal beauty. Neither tobacco breath nor yellowed teeth and fingernails are particularly appealing. Females have greater difficulty stopping smoking than males do. Perhaps males have more psychoneural, oral, visual, and manipulative substitutes.

---

[1] Jon Van, "Smoke Signals Teen Social Status," *Denver Post,* 12 April 1983.

The American Cancer Society's 1979 pamphlet, "Strategic Withdrawal from Cigarette Smoking," cites six psychological reasons for smoking that characterize smoking behavior; namely:

- *stimulation* (10 percent): the smoker that feels that he is more stimulated intellectually and can organize better by smoking;

- *handling* (10 percent): the smoker who manually experiences the handling, lighting, and smoke patterns as a form of enjoyment;

- *relaxation* (15 percent): the smoker who pleasurably enjoys a smoke after dining or for the experience itself;

- *crutch* (30 percent): the smoker who relies on smoking for emotional release of tension, stress, fear, and pressure;

- *craving* (25 percent): this smoker craves one cigarette after another and has a total dependency;

- *habit* (10 percent): this smoker has a low level of pleasure or awareness of his smoking and does so by habit.

In seeking withdrawal from smoking, these categorizations become helpful in determining quitting strategies.

think about dirty butts

female seduction

With incessant and saturation-type advertising, the cigarette companies have for years sought to capture women
in their net of addicts. The time has been ripe for inten-
sifying this marketing venture. Women seeking to be
more independent ("you've come a long way, baby"),
more feminine ("satin finish"), more alluring ("more"), or
slimmer ("slender," "light," or "slim") have caught the bait.
It appears that the source of the marketing has come
right out of the boudoir.

The female psyche is literally ripe for a release from
social- and business-world bondage. Unfortunately,
women become fair game to the entrepreneurs of tobacco
products and profit. The gruesome statistics reveal a more
than 300-percent increase in women's lung-cancer rate
since 1950. Women have indeed "come a long way" to
where they can have the opportunity to die like men. The
25,000,000 female smokers also are subject to an escalating harm from emphysema, bronchitis, and cardiovascular diseases. Other negative effects include bad breath,

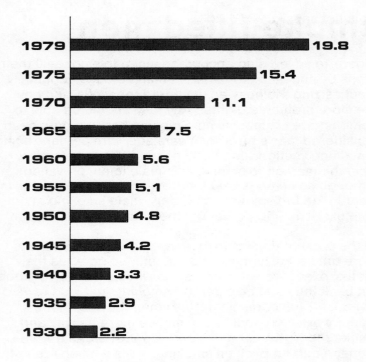

1979   19.8
1975   15.4
1970   11.1
1965   7.5
1960   5.6
1955   5.1
1950   4.8
1945   4.2
1940   3.3
1935   2.9
1930   2.2

**death rate from lung cancer
per 100,000 females**

stained teeth, odoriferous hair and clothing, wrinkles, poor skin color, and harm to unborn children and children after birth — literally made into smokers by their mothers. The infant exposed to cigarette smoke carries into this world a narrower chance for vitality and survival. The nicotine enters the smoking mother's bloodstream in about eight seconds. With this surprising rapidity, the stimulating toxin enters the placenta, the unborn baby's food supply.

A mother's love is expressed in her care for her infant. Exposing her child to tobacco smoke seems contrary to such care.

smoke-filled men

Cigarette advertising encourages men to smoke-fill their lungs by appealing to "where a man belongs," originally emphasizing the heavier, unfiltered tobaccos, and now the more profitable "lights." Any man should be able to demonstrate his machismo. Smoking has for years been considered man's territory. Years ago, with perhaps some remaining vestiges, the budding youth became a man when he learned to smoke. This male idiom prevailed, although some nags said that "every cigarette is a nail in a coffin." In the spirit of comradery, male smoking at one time exceeded 50 percent of the adult male population.

At the present time, statistics reveal that blacks smoke more unfiltered, high-tar, high-nicotine cigarettes than whites; executive and professional whites have as a group cut back the most on cigarette smoking and lean toward low-tar, low-nicotine cigarettes when they do; manual workers are more inclined to smoke more heavily and smoke the higher tar and nicotine varieties. As a whole, men are cutting back on smoking, while women are not. At present, about 35 percent of the adult male population has continued to smoke.

Smoking remains prevalent at men's clubs, conferences, meetings, sports events, etc. Unfortunately, social tolerance remains, although everyone suffers by it. Cigars and pipes remain heavily in the male province, despite their heavier intrusion upon the space of others and their greater polluting effect. Somehow, it seems easier for a male to love a pipe with a personal reflection and uniqueness, and seemingly less harm to health. A single pipe can out-pollute any cigarette in less time, if the smoker manages to keep it lit. Beyond the cheap variety, cigars retain a connoisseur status, clearly indicated by brand and name and the dignified repository of the wooden cigar box. Their prodigious outpourings when ignited, however, can literally drench indoor space with unseemly vapors.

Male perceptions of protective masculinity, leadership, and paternal roles have an association with tobacco use. The cigarette has appeared as an element of challenge; the cigar has appeared to have a forceful presence; and the pipe portrays thoughtful contemplation. For many men, smoking, chewing, dipping, or sniffing tobacco is tied in with their own view of masculinity.

The media are now beginning to pop with a new tobacco-industry assault upon human well-being by advocating "smokeless" tobacco. Such advocacy is an answer to the smoker who worries about health and the nonsmoker who avoids the intrusion of tobacco smoke. The smoker who converts to or those who take up tobacco chewing or sniffing simply trade one dangerous health hazard for another.

**pussyfootin' past
those chain-smokers**

chain-smoker

For the most part, chain-smokers are so captivated by their addiction that their lifestyle becomes one of continual indulgence. For some individuals, the necessity of eating, bathing, and defecating is an unwelcome interruption of their smoking continuum. Each chain-smoker has a definable addictive and habituated pattern. Long-term (some hours) smoking interruptions seem unbearable.

Chain-smoking sets the stage for an in-built torture under prolonged abstinence and induces attitudes strongly fettered with denial. The problem is not only a matter of the chain-smoker's health, but, also, the intense effect such smoking has upon the tolerance and well-being of others. The environment also suffers intensely, as it is flooded with unabated fumes.

A single chain-smoker is likely to puff away about two to four packs of cigarettes in the waking hours of the day. The question is, what does the smoker do when asleep? The answer is that some chain-smokers simply wake up during the night to smoke.

68

The cigarette smoker who smokes between 20 to 39 cigarettes a day has a 96 percent higher death rate than a
nonsmoker. Those who smoke 40 cigarettes per day (or
more) have a 123 percent higher death rate compared to
nonsmokers. Thus, the heavy smoker at a pack a day or
more and the chain-smoker at two or more packs a day
defy the statistical probabilities of illness and an earlier
death. Persons who have smoked least are more apt to
quit the habit, which results in a remaining number of
heavier smokers. The chain-smoker is at great risk and
increases the risk for others nearby and the burn and fire
hazard of the indoor space and its contents. The myopic
preoccupation of the chain-smoker enhances the factors
of risk that extend to automobile driving.

The message is that it is best for a smoker to quit the
habit before it strongly shackles him or her to patterns of
high-risk behavior. The smoker has most to gain in improved health, vitality, and cleaner surroundings by a
cessation of the habit. The chain-smoker has more to
gain in either quitting (a difficult task) or of not subjecting
others to a volumetric annoyance and continuum of injurious fumes. The indoor environment would also be pleased
to remain free of contamination.

gratification and territory

Smokers perceive smoking as an extension of personal territory. One study shows that smokers establish a larger sense of personal territory than do nonsmokers.[1] The smoke from the smoker literally invades the space of others, their persons, and their respiratory cavities.

Some smokers do not like to smoke in the dark, complaining that they cannot taste the smoke if they don't see it. All smoke has no boundaries until it reaches a surface it cannot penetrate. The gaseous fumes from the cigarette, cigar, or pipe tend to fill the indoor space in which they originate.

The smoker is gratified by the sight of the smoke as it moves outward. In a sense, it is both an expansion of self and the gratification of a temporary capture of space.

The smoker gains territory with noxious and toxic fumes, and the nonsmoker must either accept this territorial intrusion, flee from it, ask the smoker to stop, or stop the smoker from smoking.

---

[1] Robert G. Kunzendorf, and Joseph Denney, "Definitions of Personal Space: Smokers Versus Nonsmokers," *Psychological Reports,* vol. 50, no. 3, part 1, June 1982, p. 818.

smoking territory

Tobacco smoke has no decisive boundary until it is inter-
rupted by the body of the smoker, the nonsmoker, and
the confines of the environment.

Americans spend about 80 percent of their time indoors.
In 1980, 60 million smokers consumed over 600 billion
cigarettes, 4 billion cigars, and 12 billion pipes of tobacco.
This is a formidable amount of pollution, contamination,
health risk, and fire risk, considering that it mostly occurs
indoors. Filtration systems and all types of air-cleaning
devices and means cannot be considered as a substitute
for the elimination of indoor smoking. About 85 percent
of indoor smoking is from cigarettes, but the pollution
from cigars and pipes is proportionately greater.

Smoking not only defiles indoor air and puts at risk the
health, well-being, and cleanliness of persons and the
indoor environment, but also invades the personal territorial space and breathable air of each individual.

In an outdoor environment, the vastness of space consumes the effluents of smoking, except for localized drifts
of smoke that can intrude on others. Territorial freedom
and independence is preserved where smoking does not
occur indoors.

i am apprehensive about smokers

territorial closeness

In the territory of the home, children live within the indoor environment that can be badly polluted with tobacco smoke. They remain captive within the family, innocently breathing fume-laden air produced by a thoughtless adult. It has been suggested that heavy smoking around children may constitute a form of child abuse.

When partners who go together or live together (married or not) are a nonsmoker and a smoker, the choice can be that one or the other can always give up the partnership. The nonsmoker can find smoking intolerable and the smoker can find the nonsmoker's resentments intolerable. Smoking creates stress for the smoker and non-smoker alike (although the smoker reaches for a smoke to allay anxiety). A polluted atmosphere is a stressful territorial situation.

Being a guest or having guests visit is a territorial experience. Smoking is synonomous with the smoker. When one is a guest or receiving guests, the question is, how to separate smokers from their smoking for the well-being and comfort of others. An open discussion about the territorial aspects of tobacco smoke is likely to be the most effective route to an acceptable environment.

statistical manipulation

The Tobacco Institute, the guardian of the tobacco industry, claims there is no conclusive evidence that tobacco smoking produces cancer, emphysema, heart disease, or other major maladies. It has gleaned material from medical, technical, and scientific sources—often used out of context—to support its position. This position ignores the overwhelming results of scientific, clinical, and population studies showing the clear, statistically causative relationship between smoking and these serious diseases, shorter life spans, and a panoply of health impairments.

Industry (including tobacco manufacturers) generally takes the attitude that products not *proven* to *cause* harm can be advertised, marketed, and sold. This attitude fails to protect the consumer's health and safety. Let us ask whether the manufacture of tobacco products known or suspected of causing harm and injury to consumers, bystanders, and the environment should be allowed to continue without prescribed guidelines and reasonable standards of safety.

The tobacco industry, to gain a better public image, claims that it spends much greater sums of money for research on the effects of smoking than organizations opposed to smoking. These substantial sums are added to millions and millions of dollars spent on saturating the media with full-paged advertising. Why is this advertising and support of dubious research necessary if the tobacco industry does not seek avenues of dominance? The ploy is that each manufacturer advertises a brand for a share of a fixed market; however, this does not hold up under scrutiny. The unquestionable intent of the tobacco industry is to subdue common sense, to subvert scientific evidence, and to aggressively extend its marketing base.

the public domain

In a recent public-opinion poll covering environmental and economic issues, 77 percent of the respondents favored a clean, unpolluted environment as a prioritized effort. Nevertheless, in indoor public spaces where smoking is permitted, persons can suffer from unacceptable-to-alert levels of air pollution. The irritating, annoying, and harmful fumes of cigarettes, cigars, and pipes pollute the indoor domain of public spaces at expense to the public purse and our collective vitality.

Indoor smoking becomes a form of psychologic, emotional, and possessional harassment. People who are hypersensitive, the elderly, children, and persons with respiratory and cardiac diseases become victims of the radioactive, particulate, and gaseous effluents of tobacco smoke. Healthy nonsmokers are also affected in some measure— although the human body's recuperative ability smoothes over a number of toxic physical insults. The question is a time and exposure matter as to the degree of physiologic harm that can occur.

Everyone owns part of the public domain; yet, there are no national and few state or local restrictions on smoking in public places. In effect, by the absence of restrictions, smoking in public places is tacitly condoned as is its harm to the most vulnerable members of society as well as the most healthy. Health and environmental risk from smoking should be considered as a prime public-domain issue.

smoking pollutes us cats

indoor air pollution

The cigarette is the single, most unnecessary source of
indoor air pollution. The rate of indoor air pollution is
dependent upon the number of cigarettes being simulta-
neously smoked; the type of ingredients in the cigarette;
the burning time; the periodicity of the smoking; the
amount of exhaled mainstream smoke; the amount of
direct side-stream smoke; and contribution from the outgassing of indoor chemicals, finishes, building materials,
equipment, gas-fired appliances, carpeting, floor coverings,
furniture, and furnishings. Even books with their printed
material and plastic bindings will provide some outgassing to the space. Other variables to be considered include
air-movement patterns within the space; volume and rate
of ventilation of the indoor space; the ratio of ceiling
height to floor area; the configuration and degree of enclosure of the indoor space; contribution of fresh or polluted air from outdoors by ventilation or infiltration; selec-
tivity of the filtration used for the intake of outdoor air;
the recirculation of indoor air; the number of occupants

within the interior space and their rates of breathing and body movement; the extent of positive-field magnetic resonance; and the prevailing negative ionization.

From an individual viewpoint, the location and position of smokers within an indoor space; their fixed position or rate and type of movement; their rates of smoking; the comparative rate of smoke dilution; the directional patterns of indoor smoke; the intensity of smoke directly or indirectly received by the respiratory system of the nonsmoker or the smoker; the psychoneural, psychologic, and metabolic sensitivity of the nonsmoker and smoker; the response-avoidance factor (persons moving away or smoker extinguishing the cigarette); the level of annoyance, biologic irritation and reaction (coughing, reddened eyes, irritated nose, irritated sinus, sore throat); the deposition rate of the smoke constituents into the oral and respiratory cavities and into the bloodstream of the nonsmoker and the smoker; and the rate of natural or induced expiration from the body of such constituents all influence the amount of smoking pollution and its specific effect on each person.

Everyone is affected by states of air pollution in a different manner. From little or no sensory effects, the extent of air pollution can be biologically overwhelming and incapacitating. Everyone, in fact, is probably injured immediately—perceptibly or imperceptibly—by smoking and other harmful particulate, radioactive, and gaseous substances. The body has marvelous natural responsive defenses, but harmful substances that reside in the body for extended periods create cellular damage. The degree of harm that is slow and insidious is specific to each person and difficult to assess.

Our industrialized society's innumerable environmental and psychologic threats to human vitality and health should not confer upon smoking its right to exist. Every source of pollution harmful to humans and their environment needs to be abated and, where possible, quickly eliminated. The natural order of the world and of our bodies has only so much recovery power. Is it not reasonable that the most unnecessary sources of air pollution and biologic harm be eliminated first?

indoor spaces

Indoor spaces are rarely planned for smoking—except when nonsmoking and smoking sections are established; nevertheless, smoking is permitted in most home and building interiors. The rate of ventilation; outdoor-air quality; indoor-air quality irrespective of smoking; and the direction, amount, and intensity of ventilation flow all relate to levels of exposure, pollution, and harm caused by smoking. Smoking should occur *only* in separately isolated and separately ventilated indoor rooms and spaces. Such conditions of ventilation should avoid any intrusion of the smoke into other habitable spaces. Avoid unfiltered air recirculation. If smoking is to be allowed, the accompanying graphic layouts illustrate protective measures for locating smokers relative to indoor airflow patterns.

When discussing indoor-air quality, it is necessary to briefly outline the behavior of gases and characteristics of indoor air movement. All gaseous substances tend to fill the space they occupy. They are diluted by the total volume of air within a room, corridor, or whatever. The smaller the total volume of air within an indoor space, the higher the proportionate level of pollution that can occur from a single cigarette. Air currents within indoor spaces move from high- to low-pressure areas. Currents flow along the floor, and counterflows pass along the ceilings and through the upper parts of doorways and other openings. With solar radiation and other heat, the air currents become buoyant and rise; cooler, heavier air lies near the floor, but it is put in motion by the temperature differentials. Thus, a smoker can be a considerable distance from others, but these inductive air currents can bring the smoke-laden air into distant space occupied by others—and into their eyes, nose, throat, and lungs.

Mechanical systems often aggravate the movement of smoke from the smoker to other persons by the location of supply- and return-air ducts. The mechanical system generally distributes the smoky air (somewhat diluted by air volume and ineffective filtration) to other spaces within the building.

Building codes establish ventilation rates but, unfortunately, not levels of air quality that must be specifically maintained. Furthermore, no consideration is given under codes and regulations to the air quality of outdoor air needed for indoor ventilation.

Assuming outdoor air is reasonably clean or adequately filtered, natural or mechanical airflows can be used for its intake for indoor ventilation. In cool and cold weather, the incoming air must be air-tempered for indoor comfort. In summer, the cooling of entering outdoor air may or may not be necessary, since the rate of air movement alone tends to cool our bodies. During spring and fall (and sometimes winter and summer) when moderate outdoor air temperatures are more frequent, indoor temperature comfort is not a problem. When heat is lost from the interior during cool or cold weather, additional heat is needed to sustain a desirable indoor temperature. When summertime, air-conditioned cooling is lost, then additional, mechanical cooling is needed for exhaust ventilation. Extra energy for periods of heating, cooling, filtration replacements, maintenance, increased ventilation, and associated needs add greatly to initial and on-going energy costs where smoking occurs.

airborne smoke

Some elements of cigarette smoke are lighter and some heavier than air. In any case, the dispersion of either exhaled or side-stream smoke follows somewhat discrete, cohesive patterns. The degree and time-period rate of mixing is dependent upon the relative quiescence of the air or its rate of laminar airflow, its comparative turbulence, and the volume of the space. The nonsmoker does well to stay out of the laminar-airflow path containing dense tobacco smoke. Turbulence can be beneficial in terms of more rapid smoke dispersion and dilution. Basically, as the nonsmoker stays in the path of cleaner intake air and out of the path of exhausting or recirculative smoke, he or she can avoid the direct contaminative impact.

Quiet air conditions indicate uniform, stable, indoor-air temperatures. Laminar flow occurs between defined warm and cool air with relatively discrete (except as smoke may indicate) boundaries. Air turbulence can be caused by variant gusts of wind that enter the indoors through windows and open exterior doors. Indoor-air turbulence is particularly attributable to the amount and rate of movement in indoor space. As an example, it is very noticeable as persons move rapidly between tables at a restaurant. The air becomes more turbulent as the moving body displaces air. In contrast, smokers standing and smoking in fixed groups act as barriers to air movement. Visible tobacco clouds of smoke and their direction and state of dispersion are the best indicators of indoor places of greater smoking hazard. Nonsmokers or smokers who wish to dodge the smoke of others should observe and detect by odor the airborne smoke. The larger the indoor room space, the higher the ceiling, the greater the rate of ventilation, and the more forceful the air turbulence, the better is the opportunity to escape from harmful smoke contamination.

The ability to move about, to escape the fumes as much as possible, or to leave the smoking space is of prime importance. Fixed seating or standing spaces preclude avoidance of either drifting or dispersed airborne tobacco smoke.

neat – clean – tidy
no cigarettes

architectural strategies for commercial and institutional buildings

Where smoking is not restricted in commercial or institutional indoor spaces the nonsmoker's and smoker's exposure to tobacco smoke becomes a gamble. The size, interior volume, interior air currents, ceiling heights, mechanical systems, and furniture arrangements combine to create an environment. As smoking may take place in this environment, the number of smokers, the resultant smoke density, and the position of the occupants determine the probabilities of annoyance, irritation, and harm.

The volume, configuration, and disposition of interior furniture, furnishings, and equipment all have a defined effect on the natural convective air currents within interior architectural rooms and spaces. Interior spaces that have proportionately high ceilings and a large air volume both allow the smoke of cigarettes to rise above the general occupancy zone and also, by their volume, dilute the airborne particles.

Certain types of commercial and institutional spaces invite smoking (unless no-smoking signs are posted), such as waiting areas, conference rooms, meeting rooms, lunchrooms, corridors, and rest rooms. These are the very spaces in which people are usually in close proximity, and, thus, smoking can have an unsolicited impact upon others. If smoking is permitted in these areas, then positive control measures are needed to increase ventilation. Use selective filtration and ionization and establish separate smoking and nonsmoking areas.

Because of primary ventilation requirements, nearly all institutional and commercial structures are cooled, heated, and ventilated by air-handling systems. The location of supply, exhaust, and return air grilles is very important so that patterns of indoor airflow not only save energy by their placement away from external windows (where they are usually located) but also that nonsmokers are not caught in the return-air path when smoking prevails. The volume of ventilation air should be increased in proportion to smoking frequency and anticipated occupancy density. Exhaust systems should be located directly above smokers and smoking areas to save some energy. Exhaust systems can use heat-exchange principles: Incoming and,hopefully, fresh outdoor air can be heated by and replace the more polluted interior air.

Older buildings are apt to have mechanical systems that need attention and renovation to get better ventilation conditions where smoking exists. New buildings should be planned and designed in detail for permitted smoking. Where smoking is allowed, ventilation should be stack action, direct wind, or mechanical to the outside. A design question is whether to exhaust air from the total building volume, individual rooms, or specific interior smoking areas. It should be remembered that high ceilings in smoking spaces with an inductive, wind-turbine, or high-powered exhaust will provide better breathing conditions at nose level. It is advised that heavily textured, soft materials not be used for drapes, carpeting, or upholstery in smoking areas: They capture too much residual odor and contaminants.

It is most important that the return-air ducting of forced-air-handling systems not be contaminated with tobacco smoke or airborne contaminants. Some specific strategies to control tobacco smoke, avoid ducting contamination, and improve localized air quality in commercial buildings are given below.

Negative-ionization machines have been used in numerous office and other commercial applications for air cleaning, but the negative ions ground out quickly onto nearby wall or ceiling surfaces, creating a black-appearing residue. People are then inclined to turn the ionizer off to avoid cleaning and possibly staining the interior surfaces. This turn-off is not wise, since it means more offending smoke will be affecting human nose, sinus, throat, and lung tissue and more residues will be deposited on human hair and skin. Thus, be prepared for maintenance, or provide easy-to-clean grounding surfaces near a suspended or desk-type ionizer, or select an ionizer with a built-in surface that will ground out the ions. Consider that ducting grounds out negative ions and ionization is therefore difficult to incorporate into the mechanical filter bank.

In general, offices mixing nonsmokers and smokers have no stated smoking policy. Nonsmokers should always be seated near the air-supply side of forced-air ventilation systems and smokers near the return air. This does not remove the problem (i.e., the smoker), but it does dilute, partially clean, deodorize, and reduce the effects of the contaminated air. Ducts become more contaminated by this arrangement. I have used filters of greater-than-normal efficiency plus charcoal filters to reduce the particulates and odors. Electrostatic filters should be combined with charcoal filters downstream from the electrostatic unit to capture ozone, which is injurious to human lungs at more than three parts per hundred million parts of air. In newer installations, I have been using self-inductive electrostatic filters (dissimilar plastic screen plates generate a negative charge on particles that ground out on a positive-screen surface) combined with activated downstream charcoal filters. Charcoal filters must be changed frequently to avoid unloading the contaminants back into the air.

Enclosed, buffer spaces, sun spaces, and greenhouses can temper cool or cold incoming outdoor air; plants can partially filter it. Inasmuch as enclosed sun spaces, atriums, and greenhouses are becoming more prevalent in office buildings and other commercial and institutional structures, the heat of the sun plus passive-solar thermal storage can inductively activate substantial air movement between low air intakes and high air exhausts, abetted by efficient exhaust stacks (some are more efficient than roof wind turbines) without any mechanical assistance. Such spaces can be used for smoking when isolated from other working areas.

In cold climates, air-to-air heat exchangers can use heated indoor air to heat incoming outdoor ventilation air. Such means might provide about 70 percent of the required air tempering needed to make the air comfortable for building occupants. Look into the initial, operating, and total cost of each installation.

In theaters, office buildings, restaurants, and industrial buildings, outdoor intermission, dining, and gathering places can be provided where people can smoke or escape the crowd. Unless outdoor arcades, canopies, overhangs, awnings, and the like are designed to ventilate, the fumes from both burning tobacco and automobile exhaust can be a problem. Outdoor courts, enclosed on all or fewer sides but open to the sky can relieve to some degree adjoining offices or spaces of tobacco smoke and provide an outdoor space to smoke without bothering building occupants.

Other localized means for cleaning indoor air include portable or room-sized, electric-powered, self-contained fan and blower units that have selective filters. While the ingredients of these filters from various manufacturers are not always known, some have grapefruit-peel, activated-charcoal, chemical, or ultraviolet-light components and combinations. These devices vary in effectiveness. Some have more than one speed to facilitate a more-rapid cleaning process. The problem for more sensitive persons will be both the noise level and air velocity. Look carefully into the nature of the particular filter used. Some may not remove contaminants (such as the benzopyrenes and formaldehyde found in tobacco smoke).

One should bear in mind that smoking is not the only indoor-air contaminant. Smoking is the most serious one and one for which there should be little tolerance. Other airborne contaminants are harmful bacteria (encouraged by the positive ionization in most buildings); the introduction of polluted, outdoor air into the interior; the outgassing of synthetic materials; aerosols and sprays used to disguise smoking residues and smoke; business-processing machines; cooking; and, other equipment.

The architect and designer should address themselves to all of these problems in their selection, specification, and use of materials, methods, and devices. Even activated-charcoal air filters can be a problem, as they become loaded and can unload airborne contaminants back into the room. The maintenance of clean filters is as essential as their initial installation. In spaces where smoking is allowed, negative-ionization systems will effectively remove minute traces of the airborne particles.

A study of the interior-space plan is crucial to the convective flows of air within and between rooms. In each room or in adjoining rooms, the path of convective ventilation air should be carefully determined. It is reasonable that the highest quality of air with the least contaminants flows from nonsmoking to smoking areas. Exhaust systems, electrostatic and activated charcoal-filters, or selective, high-efficiency filters are needed for return air in the building. Generally, it is more effective to introduce fresh air from numerous peripheral sources near the floor and provide exhaust or highly efficient filtration returns at the loftiest point of the ceiling. To conserve heat during cold weather, exhaust systems should use heat recovery wheels, heat pipes, or other forms of heat exchange.

In evaluating all of these defensive and protective strategies to keep air breathable and as clean as possible for human comfort, vitality, and health, it becomes clear that considerable initial expense for systems and equipment and ongoing expense for constant maintenance is required. On the other side of the coin, if no protective means are taken, absenteeism is likely to be greater; more expensive overall cleaning or refurnishing is required; productivity is less; and discomfort, annoyance, and injury to the health of other employees is greater. This is an enormous economic burden; instead, a well-ventilated and thermally zoned smoking lounge or room might be provided for employees or management at less cost and less general debilitation of the working environment. Employees could then only smoke on breaks and lunch periods.

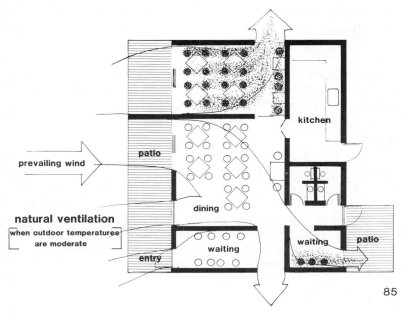

restaurant

The waiting room in a restaurant should either be completely nonsmoking or a separate (separately ventilated) waiting area should be provided. Access to dining areas should be through a no-smoking section. The smoking section should be separately enclosed and have its own exhaust and air movement system that is opposite (and a negative pressure) to the room entrance. A photocell-activated glass door is advisable but not necessary if a clear air flow is maintained through the nonsmoking dining room to and through the smoking dining where it is exhausted. The kitchen should open into the nonsmoking area to avoid contamination from the smoking area. No smoking should be permitted in the restrooms. Any outdoor dining should be planned to avoid intrusion from smoking into the building.

Air conditioning for heating and cooling and make-up air ventilation should be separate for the two dining areas. Building codes require a certain percentage of outside air for ventilation (usually about 5 to 7½ cubic feet per minute per person). This will be vastly insufficient for the smoking section. Thus air tempering energy demand requirements will be much greater for the smoking dining area.

Kitchen exhausts create a negative pressure but many codes require an outside air replenishment at a rate that offsets the amount of expelled air.

office

An advisable procedure is to prohibit smoking in waiting rooms. A less effective option is to plan the waiting room so that smoke is drawn away from nonsmokers. Another important interior consideration is to keep nonsmokers out of the path of the airborne tobacco fumes (some smokers also dislike the smoke generated by other smokers). Inasmuch as outsiders are entering the territory

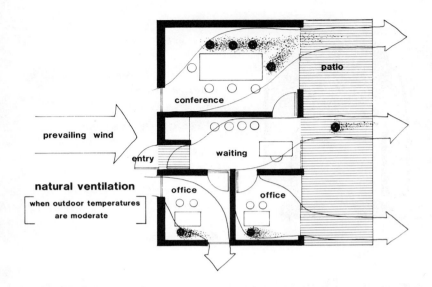

natural ventilation
when outdoor temperatures
are moderate

of persons who work within a space it would be gracious of the resident person to refrain from smoking when others are present. The next, but inferior, option is for the smoker to sit where the smoke is expelled to the outside either by flow-through ventilation or with the aid of exhaust fans. Within a conference situation, flow-through ventilation can be controlled to remove the smoke-laden air. Nonsmokers in such circumstances should be seated in the flow of incoming air and out of the path of outgoing smoke-filled air. Negative ionization can be employed to ground out smoke to the surface of dark, easily cleaned, pendant light fixtures. Soft materials used for carpet, draperies, and upholstery should be avoided where smoking occurs. Conference rooms should be exhaust ventilated.

Where smoking occurs, ventilation should be 8 to 10 times more effective than where it does not occur. Air conditioning with forced air, heating, and cooling should utilize HEPA (high efficiency particulate air), electrostatic, and charcoal filtration to reduce recirculative indoor air contamination.

**i smile when
my abode is
clear of smoke**

architectural strategies for homes and apartments

Most older homes and apartments—if they have not been made "tight" to eliminate outdoor-air infiltration— are likely to exchange outdoor for indoor air at a rate of 0.5 to 1.5 air changes per hour in winter.[1] Whether such a residence is in a non, lightly, or heavily polluted area makes considerable difference as to indoor-air quality. Smoking will quickly add to indoor pollution and poses an escalating health threat to each person in the home or apartment.

When moderate and warm weather prevails, natural or mechanical outdoor-air ventilation can be comfortably employed to dilute and carry away the offending tobacco fumes. In warm, southerly climates of the United States,

[1] American Society of Heating, Refrigerating, and Air-Conditioning Engineers, *ASHRAE Handbook and Product Directory: 1977 Fundamentals* (New York: ASHRAE, 1978), p. 21.4.

where outdoor living is common, smoking can occur out-doors with less intrusion on others. In any case, a considerate smoker should watch his or her smoke drift to prevent its effect upon others. In cold climates, smoking outdoors or in a separate, well-ventilated room is likely to have less appeal to most smokers; however, the concerned smoker may retreat (before forcing others to) to an indoor space that is as isolated as possible from others. Localized, room-type air-filtration devices can be employed to keep the indoor atmosphere as clean as possible. Children, the aged, and other persons with low vitality, illness, allergies, or high levels of sensitivity may be especially harmed by smoking. Fire risk should always be considered—particularly as a hazard for persons who may not be ambulatory.

Although these advisory thoughts apply as well to new residences and apartments, other design considerations may and should be exercised by architects and home designers. Not only smoking (the major indoor pollutant) but other outgassing materials, finishes, and equipment should be evaluated in planning and design. Basic planning to reduce or eliminate polluted air should deal with the interior volume; arrangement of closed versus open spaces; circulatory spaces such as halls, vestibules, and stairways; the placement of exterior-wall openings that can admit ventilation and daylight; and, openings, vents, and flues that exhaust air naturally or by powered means.

Outdoor air pollution levels fluctuate depending on air inversions and other conditions. The only practical way to keep indoor air as clean as possible is to not allow indoor smoking and ventilate with outdoor-air when its quality is acceptable. The larger the indoor-air volume, the more effectively that outdoor air can be selectively introduced into the interior. Beyond this process, selective, outdoor-air filtration; magnetic fields and air ionization; and other air-purificiation systems using chemical or selective-bacterial absorption or conversions can be used.

The frequency, form, and intensity of smoking that prevails are the greatest determinants of resultant air quality. Another important consideration is the direction of the smoke. Will it go into adjoining or upper bed chambers or other occupied spaces? Smoke trails provide visible evidence of the pathways of indoor-air currents and the density and rate of smoke dissipation.

Open planning has the benefit of allowing for a more rapid dissipation and dilution of the smoking effluents, but the disadvantage of less control than can occur with room containment. The exhausting of air from the entire residence should occur from a smoking room or space, and incoming fresh air (hopefully not polluted from outdoor sources) should be allowed to enter other rooms and spaces first. Halls, foyers, vestibules, and stairways can act as passageways through which tobacco smoke can travel, depending upon air movement usually occurring from internal pressure differences and through inductive temperature flow. Other internal openings also influence the smoke passage. Small, transient spaces should ideally be kept free of tobacco smoke or any other pollutant that might drift into adjoining rooms and spaces. Vestibules can be separately ventilated, and an ash receptacle can be there for extinguishing the cigarette, cigar, or pipe before the smoke is carried into the home or apartment. Any other architectural, mechanical, or interior partitioning has much to do with indoor-air quality.

I have for many years been involved with holistic-energy design of homes and commercial buildings. The following strategies have been employed for controlling the effect of smoking upon indoor residential space.

When outdoor temperatures are moderate or warm, inductive, temperature-differential ventilation can serve the entire interior of the home. Air is exhausted by the stack-action effect of the building. Outdoor air is introduced or even precooled through a basement so that, as the indoor air is warmed by the sun, occupants' body heat, and equipment, appliances, or lighting, the velocity of air ventilation is increased. Outdoor air can be brought into the building via underground areaways or ducts to use the cooling effect of the earth. This method is particularly useful in climates where nighttime temperatures are cooler than daytime temperatures. This is an energy-conserving way to remove indoor tobacco smoke from a specific room or an entire home. In cold months, when homes are buttoned up, the problem is greater.

Other ventilation methods include screened-in porches that could be used for outside smoking. Take care to selectively close sliding-door or window openings to prevent smoke from entering indoor spaces.

Powered exhaust ventilation can be used for any specific room or for a whole house to remove airborne smoke. Bathroom and kitchen exhaust fans can help somewhat for ventilation, but bathrooms and kitchens are poor places for smoking if other occupants may be in or using such spaces.

Electrostatic air cleaners can remove particulates, and downstream, activated-charcoal filters can be added to remove ozone generated at times by the electrostatic grid. Such filtration systems should be serviced frequently relative to the amount of indoor smoke passing through them.

To prevent ductwork contamination, use a centralized, negative-ion system with terminals in various rooms and a positive-resonance magnetic-field generator with ceiling or wall plates to capture the effluents from tobacco smoking.

Outdoor patios, terraces, and other covered or uncovered spaces are not only adaptable to outdoor living but also to persons who want to smoke. If other persons are using such spaces, the considerate smoker should see which way the outdoor breezes are going to keep smoke away from others.

A special smoking room or space can be a den, study,

utility room, workroom, or even the garage that can be well ventilated and isolated from other general living spaces.

Well-ventilated atriums, sun spaces, and greenhouses cut off from living areas by tight-fitting doors can serve as temporary smoking places. The faster the rate of natural or powered ventilation and the less smoking that occurs, the more readily such spaces will be made habitable for nonsmokers.

Another concept seldom used in this country is the roof garden or deck for outdoor living and enjoyment. While smoking remains an intrusive habit, it becomes much less so when people smoke outdoors.

Unroofed courts that penetrate the building configuration offer a similar opportunity for the smoker to breathe some fresh air while polluting his or her lungs. Sliding doors or other openings that open into the building should be closed where smoking occurs.

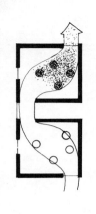
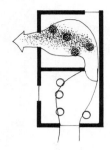
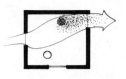

natural ventilation for indoor rooms

with prevailing wind when outdoor
temperatures are moderate

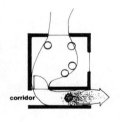

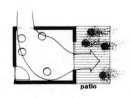

corridor

corridor

patio

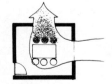

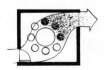

natural ventilation for indoor rooms

with prevailing wind when outdoor
temperatures are moderate

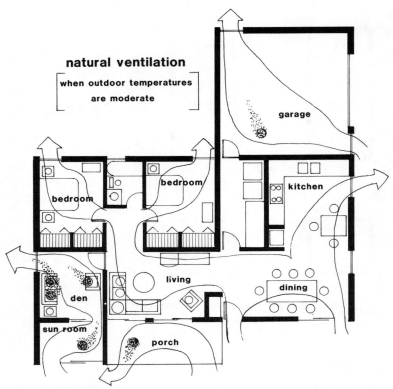

natural ventilation

when outdoor temperatures
are moderate

garage

bedroom

bedroom

kitchen

living

den

dining

sun room

porch

residences

Wherever people reside, a separate room, outdoor or
semi-outdoor space (balconies, porches, verandas), or
outdoor space (patios, terraces, courtyards, balconies)
should prevail to accommodate persons who smoke. The
location, size, and character of air passage openings are
critical to the direction and effectiveness of air flow patterns. The location of openings, air movement, and volume
of smoking has much to do with the on-going and residual
effects of airborne smoke.

The more separate and isolated from other spaces that
indoor smoking may occur, the less smoke pollution will
affect other indoor spaces. Smoking should not occur in
corridors or places where it can drift into various rooms.

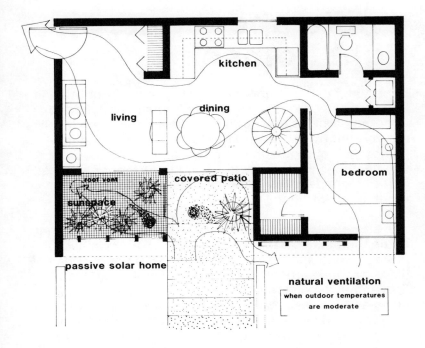

kitchen

living

dining

covered patio

bedroom

roof vent

sunspace

passive solar home

natural ventilation

when outdoor temperatures
are moderate

During cold weather when indoor spaces are buttoned up, a mechanical exhaust, smoke-absorbing ash trays, or one of the more efficient air cleaning machines can serve to reduce the density of smoke contaminants.

As mentioned in this book, well-ventilated attached green-houses and sunspaces that can be closed off from the general indoor living and sleeping areas can be used as a temporary place for smoking. Avoid soft fabrics where smoking occurs.

a note about energy-tight homes

Energy-tight homes enhance the radon concentration in indoor air. Radon-decay products become attached to airborne particles and surfaces. The indoor radon levels, as reported by Dr. Edward Martell, are about ten times higher than outdoors in summer. Closing the house or building up in winter to retain warmth further enhances indoor radon levels and the need for ventilation to reduce radon concentrations.

The strategy to minimize and control the lethal potential of the radioactive particles is control of radon influx, planned ventilation, and selective filtration of dust particles, fibrous aerosols, and tobacco-smoke particles. Preventative measures include sealing basement surfaces and crawl spaces around cracks, drains, or other floor openings to reduce radon levels. Another solution is an air-to-air heat exchanger that heats incoming, fresh, filtered air with outgoing, exhaust air. Such devices, however, are not cheap, require installation and operational energy, and are likely to be only about 70 percent efficient. Attached greenhouses, sun spaces, and atriums can be designed to admit and temper outside air. These spaces can use vegetation to improve filtration, oxygenation, and humidity.

sealed buildings

Many high-rise and low-rise buildings are completely sealed and have integral ventilating systems. Some systems are centralized, others serve thermally zoned areas, and some have through-the-wall conditioners that serve individual room spaces.

From the standpoint of smoking the questions that must be asked are: What are the air changes per hour, the source of intake air, interior spatial volumes, the percentage of return air, the distribution layout, and the effectiveness of the filtration? The frequency of the filter change and the relative amount of smoking that occurs indoors is critical to the overall air quality.

Inasmuch as the internalized sealed building has a definable inbuilt air distribution system, the systemic constancy of the ventilation makes it easier to locate nonsmokers out of the direct return air path of the tobacco smoke. The interior volume smoke air dilution factor is dependent upon the air volume and rate of air change.

A negative aspect of the sealed building is not only the energy wasting dependency upon the mechanical systems but the extenuating noise level of the operating equipment. Carpet, drapes, soft upholstery in furniture, or whatever tends to retain tobacco odors for prolonged periods due to the lack of a more intensive degree of air movement.

Through all seasons, and all periods of daily occupancy, persons within the building become pawns to the mechanical ventilating system. How well they fare under the closed system of personal containment depends upon the concern and skill of the mechanical engineer as well as the architect who creates the interior air volumes.

natural airflows

Outdoor wind creates an air pressure upon the windward side of a building. As the air moves around and over the building, a negative pressure is induced on the side and rear. Windows, vents, and openings facing the wind receive direct, positive air pressure and, on the sides or rear, a negative (low) pressure. The building is ventilated by the rate and intensity of this airflow through its interior spaces. The configuration, form, texture, and details of a building influence the wind-flow pattern as it enters through building openings. Interior airflow is affected by ceiling heights, openings between floors (such as stair-wells and light wells), and how roof vents, roof stacks, or skylight openings may create inductive upward airflows that exhaust by stack action. In effect, the building itself acts to exhaust air in the manner of a chimney. The warmer the outgoing air and cooler the incoming air, the more rapidly (depending on size of intake-air and exhaust openings) the interior airflow can be inductively exhausted by using the solar heat of an attached sun space or with a ventilating roof stack.

Inductive ventilation is generally accomplished by changes in air pressure induced by temperature or inductive, external air movement and air pressure. Air becomes more bouyant as it is heated. Secondary air currents are impelled more rapidly by the movement of primary air currents. Air is heated by the sun and internal heat sources such as lights, people, and equipment. The more quickly that the air is warmed, the more rapidly it will rise and be inductively exhausted. Wind moving across the roof stack or roof configuration can inductively, by negative pressure, increase the exhaust ventilation.

For the most part, wind direction and intensity have a prevailing seasonal pattern influenced by site and the architecture of the building and placement, size, and type of building openings. Screening can reduce wind and general airflow by as much as 40 percent. Optimized cross ventilation that flows diagonally across interior spaces ventilates interior space better than the usual center-of-the-wall placement. See drawings in the preceding chapters.

Although wind has a prevailing direction, it can be capricious. In a home, shifts in wind can be met by an appropriate response; namely, opening and closing of windows, vents, and doors. If smoking occurs outdoors, it should be away from exterior openings that would bring the fumes into the building. If smoking is allowed indoors, it should always be downstream from nonsmokers and closest to the outgoing air. The preceding illustrations show the various indoor-space-use situations that reduce the objectionable odors and effects of smoking upon nonsmokers.

mechanical airflows

Various types and forms of electrically powered fans and blowers give more positive control over indoor airflows than by natural, convective, wind-pressured, and inductive means.

Appropriate filters are advised for incoming air. When smoking indoors, smokers should be close to an air exhaust. A nonsmoking area should be vented every half-hour, but, in a smoking area, a complete air change should occur about every two to five minutes, depending on the amount of smoking.

It becomes quite clear that smoking demands an excessive amount of energy use. Furthermore,when it is cold outdoors, the rapid loss of indoor heat and physical comfort by exhaust has to be quickly counteracted by quickly heating volumes of incoming air. This wastes even greater amounts of energy. In hot areas, a similar experience requires the cooling of incoming air with a corresponding waste of energy. In all of the natural-airflow illustrations, it is advised that primary- and supplementary-exhaust systems and the air-tempering of intake air as required be provided. Exhausts should always be located in smoking areas furthest away from nonsmokers. The incoming ventilation should always cross the greatest area of the nonsmoking section. In restaurants or other facilities with exhaust fans (such as rest rooms), care should be exercised that other power exhausts provided for smoking sections will maintain a negative pressure.

It is most desirable that fresh, filtered, incoming ventilation air have a positive pressure; or, better yet, a positive, mechanical-airflow pressure for the nonsmoking or other spaces (such as computer rooms) intended to be kept smoke-free. All smoking sections should have outgoing airflow and a negative pressure. These measures will benefit the smoker as well as the nonsmoker by reducing discomfort, minimizing air pollution relative to entire indoor spaces, increasing the ventilation of indoor spaces for improved health and well-being, and reducing tobacco-smoke odors.

air purification

The consumer market is being saturated by a host of room-type air cleaners. It is impossible to determine the relative merits of the least-to-most expensive units for improving indoor-air quality. At best, even the most efficient units cannot compete, on a relative air-purity basis, with a highly concentrated continuum of smoking. The primary key to successful time-period air cleaning is the nature of the filter, how frequently it will be changed, and how many air changes the unit can provide by the process of interior-air recirculation. The efficiency and size of the filtration media plus the volume of air passing through it are central to its ability to capture the gaseous, particulate, and radioactive particles of the tobacco smoke. Smoke visibility and odor are not good indicators of air quality except for larger airborne particles that are less harmful than a proliferation of small, nonvisible particles, which are not easily expelled from the respiratory system.

The great popularity of air cleaners attests to the desire of persons to achieve a pleasant and breathable indoor atmosphere. Unfortunately, most of the small units do not possess adequate filter size, selective media effectiveness, or cubic-feet-of-air-per-minute delivery. For the most part, the consumer is subject to less-than-expected benefits. Persons are also not apt to change filters as often as needed because of inconvenience and cost.

A major factor of all units is noise level of operation. For anyone with the least sensitivity to noise, virtually all units range from annoying to intolerable. Most units have no recorded decibel rating of sound generated. In this regard, as to performance and generated-noise level, standards and product labeling should be a consumer-protection requirement.

Unfortunately, the proliferation of room air "purifiers" (a poor designation for many) may counter the action of many smokers who would make a greater attempt to stop their habit. Furthermore, units that recirculate air within a room space are not likely to exchange more than 50 percent of the total air volume in two or more hours. With continual smoking in a room space, perceptible odors and imperceptible contamination are likely to remain despite the constant operation of the unit. Larger, more-sophisticated purification units with or without ionization or electronic capability, charcoal, HEPA filters, or ultra-violet lamps are most likely to have better performance characteristics but are much more expensive.

Cessation of the smoking habit where possible is certainly a preferred choice, as it eliminates the need for air-purification equipment, its necessary continual maintenance, the energy needed to run it, and remaining maintenance for cleanup of the spent tobacco. It should be noted that a nonsmoking environment saves 30 to 50 percent in cost over a smoking environment requiring ongoing mainte-nance.

This book does not purport to endorse the air-purification unit of any manufacturer but only to present information germane to each form of indoor-air quality control. A clear distinction should be made between the use of outdoor-air ventilation (filtered or unfiltered) versus recir-culative indoor-air filtration. A pertinent question in the use of outdoor ventilation is how clean or polluted it is for indoor ventilation use.

filters

Filters come in many sizes, densities, and thicknesses, and have specific material characterisitics and disposition of filtering media. The principal effectiveness of a filter depends upon the size and configuration of the openings through which the air must pass, as well as the path and materials' interception of airborne particulates, absorption of gases, and the electrostatic and ionization properites of the materials or energizing of the filter screens or media. Filters can be replaceable or cleanable.

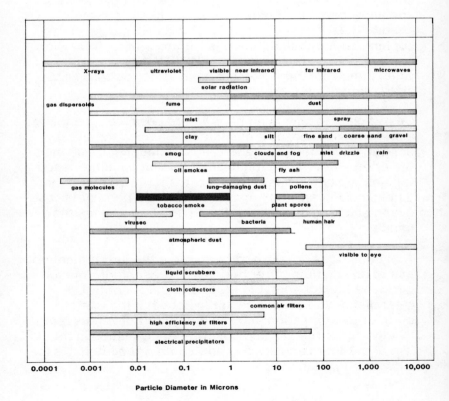

Particle Diameter in Microns

conventional filters

These will capture only the larger, airborne particles of about ten microns or greater in size. (A micron is one-millionth of a meter.) Because these filters have relatively large openings between natural, synthetic, or glass fibers, they require minimal forced-air and minimal air-pressure drop in passing through the filter.

self-activating electronic filters

A filter is available that consists of several layers that induce electrical charges on particles that pass through them. The air first passes through a polypropylene screen that negatively charges the forced-air particles; centralized acrylic rods and polyurethane control filter-elements become positively charged and, subsequently, air that moves through a final, polypropylene screen is negatively charged to pick up positive, soiled particles loosened from the central member. Thus, the dissimilar screens create a filter without ozone-producing disadvantages, a relatively high level of airborne, particulate capture, and no need for electric energy. Performance is reputed to be better than conventional electronic filters.

high-efficiency particulate air (HEPA) filters

These are claimed to be more efficient for particulate-filtering cigarette and other smoke. Special attention should be given to the design: As the filter picks up greater amounts of dirt, the filter efficiency improves as the interception of tobacco smoke or other effluents have to be forced through smaller, more resistant openings. Claims are made that the effectiveness in capturing small particles in the air is greater than for electrostatic (electrically charged) air-filtration elements. HEPA filters require greater fan horsepower because of the surface resisitance of the filter.

electrostatic filters (electrically powered)

Such filters consist of an open, metallic screen that electrically charges incoming, airborne particles. The charged particles are grounded out within the next stage of the filter. Such filters must be carefully handled in the cleaning operation, so as to not damage the electrical connections. Such filters are most effective when clean and rapidly lose their efficiency as the cells within the charged plates of the filter become restricted with increasing, retained particulates. A principal disadvantage is the production of ozone, which substantially increases as the unit becomes clogged and a greater number of small short circuits develop on the grid. Charcoal filters should be used with electrostatically powered filters to capture ozone and odors.

charcoal filters

Such filters come in a number of diverse densities and prescriptive designs for various kinds of applications. Activated charcoal has a particular affinity for the absorption of airborne gases and elimination of odors. Replacement or activated-charcoal renewal becomes essential before the filter media tends to unload its contamination back into the airstream.

**smoking is a pain
in my cat gut**

economics of smoking at the work place

The costs to a business that hires smokers can be considerable. The dollar losses, in terms of reduced productivity, greater absenteeism and disability, extra maintenance, increased furniture depreciation, higher premiums for health and fire insurance, and lower employee morale, combine to make the employment of smokers a hidden economic burden for many businesses.

A recent article gave the following percentages of savings a business could expect by hiring only nonsmokers and prohibiting smoking on company property[1]:

- up to 10 percent in salaries and wages

- 30 percent in health- and fire-insurance premiums

---

[1] William Weiss, "Smoking: Burning a Hole in the Balance Sheet," *Personnel Management,* vol. 13, no. 5, pp. 24-29.

- 50 percent in furniture depreciation

- 50 percent in cleaning expenses

- 75 percent in disability benefits

The article gives additional statistics concerning savings; for example, female smokers as a whole are absent from work 45.1 percent more often than their nonsmoking counterparts; for men the differential is 56.8 percent. For male smokers between the ages of 17 and 44, the absentee rate climbs to 83.3 percent more than their nonsmoking peers.[2]

Time lost to smoking on the job is estimated at about 30 minutes per day for cigarette smokers, 55 minutes per day for pipe smokers. Based on an eight-hour workday, about 6.25 percent and 11.25 percent of the work year, respectively, is lost in the smoking ritual.[3]

Another factor for businesses to consider is that tobacco smoke is a severe air contaminant that requires dramatically increased ventilation: as much as ten times the ventilation required for nonsmoking areas.[4] This translates into increased energy demand. Energy budgets should include smoking as a prime cost. The additional initial, operational, and maintenance costs of mechanical equipment to handle the added energy demand should all be priority budget items.

Smoking can be damaging or deleterious to instruments, laboratory and computer equipment, and valuable documents. Smoking contaminates the duct systems of buildings, air-type solar collectors, and other equipment that uses return air from interior space. Smoking requires the frequent maintenance of air, electrostatic, and charcoal filters or mechanical systems. Merchandise (particularly

---

[2] Ibid.   [3] Ibid.
[4] *Energy Inform: Designing for Energy Conservation,* by the AIA Res. Corp. with Syska and Hennessey (Washington, D.C.: AIA Res. Corp., 1978), p. 7.

"soft goods") can be readily damaged by tobacco smoke and can be unsalable, as merchants know only too well.

Some individuals will complain that they cannot work effectively unless they are allowed to smoke, and, obviously, many competent and outstanding individuals do smoke. The simplest solution is for all smokers to be isolated and that space be independently ventilated so that smoke fumes cannot enter the domain of others.

It costs money to make special provision for smokers to smoke without affecting others. The old smoking cars of yesteryear on steam passenger trains were a case in point. A compensating viewpoint is that, as separate smoking rooms or highly controlled, well-ventilated smoking sections are provided, the great savings in direct and indirect costs for maintenance of indoor space and health vastly offset the special smoking provision costs. Businesses that employ only nonsmokers solve the problem initially and without maintenance costs.

The fact that his or her smoking habit could deny a person employment could be a powerful inducement for that individual to stop smoking.

Another economic factor businesses should consider is that the majority of people are nonsmokers. Clients, customers, and business patrons can be annoyed, irritated, or repelled by a smoking receptionist, clerk, salesperson, attendant, waiter, or other employee.

Every business is obligated to protect its employees. Smoking is the most common intruder upon the space of others (nonsmokers and smokers alike) and their person and possessions. An employer concerned about his or her employees and productive and economic factors should give heed to the smoking problem. This concern should extend to travel in vehicles by more than one employee.

Occasionally, employees sensitive to or made ill by workplace tobacco smoking have successfully brought suit against their employer to provide a smoke-free work environment. Hopefully, legal redress may result in more protective laws for a cleaner work environment with the benefit of breathable air. If it became common for smokers to be paid less in proportion to the harm and disruption they cause to others and impose upon the work place, many would quit their habit or reduce it so that it did not intrude on the work environment.

burned out

Cigarettes cause more burns than any other source. Clothes, bedclothes, floor coverings, furniture, drapes, counters, and personal belongings all succumb to superficial or irreparable cigarette burns. The high burning temperature of the cigarette plus its sustained combustion creates a constant fire hazard where smoking occurs.

Smokers are particularly prone to be careless about the burns and fires that they create. This propensity toward hazard is caused by the smokers' preoccupation with their habit, as well as its constant demand. The attrition rate is exceptionally high for carpet, vinyl, and wood flooring. Burns escalate in proportion to the number of smokers, the frequency of their smoking, and their distraction to other things while smoking.

Scorches and burns do not necessarily ruin the utility of a material or a product but invariably injure its appearance. Burns injure or destroy documents, furniture, furnishings, and attire. Invaluable records have been lost to burns and fire caused by smoking. Unquestionably, if all of the costs for repair, replacement, and irreplaceable loss of papers and possessions could be so calculated, it would be an astronomical figure. National property loss to fires caused by smoking in 1981 exceeded 300 million dollars. Room fires and content loss, sometimes with loss of life or body burns, can especially occur where smoking occurs in bed at home, in hotels, in nursing homes, and in dormitories.

marketing and risk

The tobacco industry, like most businesses, seeks to sustain its market and optimize operations and profits. The matter of health, composure, and a clean environment does not hang heavy on the tobacco industry's conscience. Its guilt is partially assuaged by purported scientific research on the safety (or harm) of smoking.

As fortune would have it, smokers are eager to reduce their risks and are ready for safer cigarettes or alternatives to smoking. Unfortunately, the evidence is strong that smokers of low-tar and low-nicotine cigarettes simply smoke more to maintain their addictive dosage and are exposed further to the unknown hazards of taste enhancers and other chemical additives with unknown health consequences. The tobacco industry has benefitted by smokers who keep on smoking with misplaced confidence, lesser-quality tobacco, cheaper ingredients, and increased sales volume to smokers smoking more to satisfy their addiction with lower-dosage cigarettes.

Cigar, pipe, snuff, and chewing tobaccos appeal to the smoker as safer alternatives; however, these alternatives have their own health risk. The consumer who has a desire is always beguiled by avenues that sustain addictions and gratifications but appear to reduce risks. Tobacco marketing and advertising are willing to oblige.

the money question

Money makes the world go around. It is a universal need. There is little doubt that, if the entire smoking industry were suddenly eliminated, vast economic displacement would occur. From soil to vending machine, dependent industries and services would become unemployed. However, it should be considered that everyone would subsequently be in better health, enjoy a cleaner indoor environment, and be free of smoking odors and the major cause of indoor and outdoor fire. Life would be immeasurably more pleasant. The displacement from a tobacco economy to a more rational one that could provide creative, wholesome (at least more so) constructive gratifications would not only do more for our remaining generation, but all of the generations that follow.

It doesn't take much vision to comprehend a freer, safer, and more livable world without the aggressive impacts of tobacco smoking. To be truly free, a society cannot cast the burdens of a minority upon a majority.

Money is an important transactional element, but to waste it on a nefarious product as well as time, cleanliness, health, and energy does not appear to be a reasonable destiny for a civilly concerned society.

All cigarette manufacturers are diversifying. When you buy baby food or a cake of soap, you are likely to be supporting some element of the tobacco industry—be it only the advertising agency. The greater the diversification of the tobacco industry, the less it can feel any economic burden if it loses a portion of its ventures. Unfortunately, because of its addictive demand upon the user, tobacco products are a lucrative, less-market-sensitive, and more profitable business than many other consumer items. Notice that in diversification, the tobacco barons are choosing consumer necessities and higher-return products.

Taxation is a form of monetary control. Taxes derived from harmful and sometimes dangerous products have been channeled into beneficial constructive uses, but is it not better to remove support from such products by excessive taxation and restrictive legislation so persons will be impelled to use their money for more worthwhile purposes?

The huge, billion-dollar tobacco industries can well stand the brunt. They can invest their money into any other venture, assist the tobacco farmer, their personnel, and all of those suppliers and handlers of their product with new product and investment alternatives. If the tobacco industry has any human conscience invested in people more than product, it will accelerate rather than dampen its own lead into profitable, wholesome ventures.

cigarette machines

Cigarette machines tucked in every corner of our commercial establishments and public places are an open invitation to youth. The unattended machine asks for no ID card.

The lighted display of the packages, the ease for anyone to procure a product that can be more harmful than a number of FDA-regulated drugs is a matter of irrationality. The prevalence of the cigarette machine is an insistent point-of-sale device. It conveys the message that smoking is condoned where the machine is located as well as any time of day or night, a readiness to dispense its dangerous commodity.

We live in a world of machines that continue to crowd out our human space. Cigarette machines are not the only intrusive mechanism but they can be rated as the most deplorable. Proprietors and managers of all businesses and institutions should give more thought to the consequences of cigarette machine installations. Even if they disregard the human implications, how about the injury they invite to their own establishments?

**smoking ruffles
my dignity**

manners

Manners are social customs that tend to keep us pleasantly aligned with each other. Predictable, nonoffensive, behavioral repetitions in voice, body movement, dress, and attitude toward others preserves an equanimity. Social conflicts are reduced, understanding is enhanced, and the discipline of the manner becomes a behavioral symbol that describes nonaggression. Measured in this light, let us consider smoking.

All forms of smoking are aggressive as the smoke knows no boundaries and invades the space of others, pollutes the indoor air with an odoriferous stench, drops ashes, and leaves a mess of spent butts. Only the patient tolerance of nonsmokers (and most smokers) allows the habit to continue in homes, cars, and places of business. Smoking anywhere others gather can create minor or major conditions of stress. Smoking only increases the probability of social conflicts and of tarnished understanding. Harsh, acrid drifts of cigarette smoke, the heavy suffocation of cigar smoking, and the overwhelming aromatic encapsulation that occurs from ignited pipe tobacco seem dismally out of place in a well-mannered society.

The thrust of most cigarette ads is to make smoking socially acceptable. There is a rising tide of social unacceptability and rejection of smoking in public and many private places. The tobacco industry fears that smoking might become regarded as antisocial. How any civilized society spending 80 percent of its time indoors with increasingly dense gatherings and assemblies might still tolerate smoking in any indoor space defies human logic. In any terms, smoking is antisocial, assuming that we try to treat others with concern, respect, and in a well-mannered way. In all aspects, smoking where other persons are present in indoor space is inconsiderate.

Persons of taste, self-respect, and thoughtfulness of others do not pick their nose, spit, or create loud or objectionable noises in public and generally behave in a seemly way. On the other hand, as soon as they light up a cigarette, cigar, or pipe, they offend their own sensibilities and those of others and, in addition, pollute the indoor air, contaminate or burn holes in furnishings and furniture, and leave a pile of spent butts or tobacco.

We spend a good deal of our lives learning social grace. In contrast, tobacco smoking is a social disgrace.

smokers protecting nonsmokers

Smokers can do more than nonsmokers to protect the nonsmokers' composure, vitality, cleanliness, and health. Not smoking when nonsmokers are present is the first mark of consideration. A less considerate stance is for smokers to smoke with discretion; that is, to minimize smoking and to smoke near exhaust fans, outgoing air, or places where ventilation is optimized when indoors.

Responsible smokers should keep their habit under observation. The questions to consider are: How much smoke is getting into the air? Which way does the smoke drift? Is the ash receptacle placed where tobacco smoke doesn't go toward others? Is the spent cigarette or cigar butt or pipe tobacco completely and promptly extinguished? Is the stenchful mess of spent tobacco quickly removed? If you transact with others indoors in your work, it is inconsiderate to light up when others are present. If it is your space, others put up with your behavior. If it is not your space, it is an affront to light up. Responsible smokers consider what their smoke is doing.

It is interesting to note that the Tobacco Institute claims that side-stream smoke does not harm healthy individuals. But a vast number of people are not healthy. The amount of side-stream smoke inhaled and its effect upon anyone, healthy or unhealthy, depends upon how much smoking occurs.

i relax when nobody smokes

sensitivity

Our individual sensitivities protect us and others. The most sensitive person in a group often saves the lives of others. A sensitive nose can detect a fire, an odor that warns of danger, the intensity of air pollution, or the safety of fresh and breathable air.

Tobacco smoke contains poisons that can be ultimately lethal and, even with localized air dilution, are not only unpleasant but have harmful amounts of toxins. Should not air quality be determined by the most sensitive noses in a society rather than by the atrophied nasal receptors of the average person? Our society is so beset with chemical fumes, tobacco smoke, automobile exhaust, perfumes, lotions, and odoriferous aerosols (usually to mask other odors) that people lose a sensitive discrimination in smell. Not to be overlooked, however, is the carbon monoxide that robs the blood of oxygen. It has no odor whatsoever, yet can be lethal.

Hay fever or asthma affect as much as 15 to 17 percent of the U.S. population. Studies of passive and active smoking have shown that people with allergies, especially those with rhinitis or asthma, may be more sensitive to the nonspecific, noxious effects of cigarette smoke than healthy individuals.[1]

smokers protecting themselves

The greatest protection smokers can secure for themselves is to completely stop smoking. The next measure is to drastically cut to a minimum their amount of smoking.

It is not demonstrated that low-tar, low-nicotine, and filtered cigarettes will necessarily lessen smoking health risks. Bypass-filter cigarettes can record low-tar, low-nicotine levels on smoking machines, but, in actuality, the pressure of smokers' lips substantially closes apertures and adjusts the puffing rate; thus, more tar and nicotine is consumed than the ratings indicate. The cigarette manufacturer is not constrained in adding any ingredients to their product. There is a probability that flavor enhancers—particularly for low-tar and low-nicotine cigarettes—or other additives may increase their harmfulness.

the great outdoors

The more that smokers take action to protect themselves, the more that they will protect others. By smoking *outdoors*, smokers will secure a number of health and environmental advantages. A fundamental advantage is direct dilution of the tobacco fumes by wind and air movement. Also, smokers will benefit more by the fresh air than by indoor air likely to be contaminated by radioactive decay that attaches to smoke particles and outgassing from materials and equipment. Indoor air is likely also to be vitiated by lack of oxygen and a surplus of carbon dioxide from human exhalation and indoor combustion.

---

[1] American Cancer Society, *Dangers of Smoking,* p. 49.

When weather may not permit, smokers can serve their interest in their own health and nonsmokers' by smoking in an isolated indoor room or space that is separately and well ventilated. Smoking in an outdoor environment protects the interior. Smoking in an isolated indoor space protects adjoining indoor spaces. As much as possible in any climate, outdoor spaces developed for living and activity in the interest of well-being enjoy less cost than full architectural enclosures, no cost for mechanical climatization, and freedom to commune with nature. Opportunities for any degree of weather and climate protection can exist between the fully open outdoor garden, terrace, patio, and deck and partial enclosure with architectural overhangs, full roofs, canopies, and various degrees of walled-in or screened-in enclosures. Provision for natural ventilation can always be enhanced by induced-air convection and control over wind motion by architectural and landscaping means. With good air-movement design, spaces that are more fully open to the natural environment can vastly reduce and even eliminate much of the harm caused by smoking. Overhead canopies, deep roof overhangs, and awnings that are tight to a building can create relatively still air conditions that retain smoke. The answer is to leave a space between the outdoor covering and the building or to use forms, shapes, and stack-action ventilators to take away the fumes. Porches and arcades are likely to retain more of the smoky air unless ventilated, but any place outdoors is better than in. Care should be exercised so outdoor smoke does not flow indoors.

Bridging the outdoors and indoors requires a design that protects the smokers and the nonsmokers who wish to be in the company of smokers. As spaces gain a greater degree of enclosure, such as enclosed porches, sun rooms, sun spaces, greenhouses, or atriums that can be closed off completely from indoor living and activity areas, the success in maintaining a healthful atmosphere in the presence of smoking will depend largely on ventilation design. Air tempering, using the sun for heat and the earth and atmosphere for cooling, should not be neglected in the interest of energy conservation, minimal utility energy demand, and the vitalizing benefits of these natural elements.

Everyone loves the great out-of-doors, the question is, how to make best use of its wonderful bounties? Even on those days when air pollution occurs, smoking outdoors will be less harmful than if experienced in the confines of indoor space.

**i see you coming –
you're smoking – i'm going**

nonsmokers
protecting themselves

Smokers can do the most about the plight of nonsmokers, but nonsmokers can take measures to protect
themselves. Certain environments literally invite or cater
to smokers, such as cocktail lounges, hotels, sports are-
nas, restaurants, bowling alleys, and events such as conferences, seminars, business meetings, and social gatherings. By not going to such places or functions, nonsmokers can set a precedent accompanied by a written
message to the functionees as to why they are not attend-
ing. Without letters of protest, people in charge will retain
the idea that smoking is customary and acceptable.
Wherever nonsmokers see an ashtray or receptacle they
should not go. A defensive measure is to move ashtrays
or receptacles to out-of-the-way places before the
smokers get there and light up.

Avoidance techniques include a careful survey of each
indoor environment to find out the most smokeless corner

or place of escape. If asked by smokers whether you object to their lighting up, be kind but firm in saying "yes" if you really don't want them to. Thin-layered silk or wool scarves can be helpful to use as nasal filters. As the fibers become electrostatically charged by air movement, they ground out some of the offending cigarette-smoke particles. In any case, in a place from which you cannot escape, stand or sit near an *incoming* air supply; or, where possible, increase the ventilation by opening a door, window, or vent. When you are with others and another person or persons in the group light up, ask the smokers to move outdoors and give them the reasons for doing so. Most smokers will apologize and not light up.

In general, smokers do not want to annoy, irritate, or have their smoke cause a problem for someone else. The question is how to elicit their response and concern. They will not, because of smoking being such a widespread and common habit, normally give due consideration to the harm they foist upon their own children, persons with serious respiratory or vascular problems, or anyone else.

It is interesting to note that more and more persons offering to share apartment space with another will not accept a smoker.

more strategems for nonsmokers

If you are deeply concerned about your health, vitality, and a clean indoor environment (as well as for your family), live and vacation in cities, towns, or states that prohibit or adequately control smoking in public places, including restaurants, motels, hotels, shops, stores, offices, and places of recreation. If you are ultrasensitive, allergic, or have a respiratory, circulatory, or hormonal disease affected by smoking, such a course of action can make your life more pleasant and less risky. If you live in a city, town, or state without legislative controls over smoking, you can only employ avoidance and control strategies of your own making.

Making your home a nonsmoking sanctuary. Persuade your friends and relatives to do the same. Show your appreciation for their cooperation. Put up a no-smoking sign or symbol on your front-entry door, in your car, and at your work place. If you run a business, set up protective measures for employees and customers. Patronize firms or individuals who prohibit smoking intrusion. Let them know why you give them your patronage.

Give no-smoking parties or hold no-smoking events. Get publicity for your effort. Business people can employ such strategies as a form of receptive advertising. Make the cigarette ads appear ridiculous. Have a no-smoking costume ball depicting the absurdity of smoking. Use imagination with human-concern appeals. Have some fun. Some smokers will lay back and listen. Hopefully, they will quit and get into the swing of things.

Hotels and sports events are notorious in allowing smoking. Protest to the hotels, motels, and sports-gathering places where smoking is allowed. Encourage them to clean up their environment and get more business from the majority—which is nonsmoking. Discourage smoking at all events with printed announcements stating "no smoking." Such stances should apply at every level of private or public affairs. No-smoking sections at banquets, conferences, meetings, and other gatherings are a good start but in most cases are not fully adequate. Indoor spaces simply are not designed to handle smoking and, if they were, they could only do so by determined, protective design.

Persons who are not militant but concerned can accomplish a large measure of protection by a sustained level of defensive awareness. When a smoker lights up, move away. Find pockets of fresher, indoor air or retreat to the outdoors. If you feel vocal, tell the smoker why you are avoiding the tobacco smoke. In gourmet and fine food restaurants, ask to be seated away from smokers, even though a no-smoking section may prevail. Further, tell the maitre d' or hostess to be prepared to relocate you out of the path of any drifting smoke. Patronize family food restaurants that have no-smoking areas. In particular have your children seated away from smokers. Let the children know why.

If you are sensitive, allergic, or have a respiratory ailment, let persons know beforehand that smoking seriously affects you.

legislation

The tobacco industry undermines the fundamental legislative process in this country. In effect, the industry, representing a nefarious product, impairs the democratic judgment of our legislators by implication and duplicity.

However, if legislators care enough about people and truly care about the welfare, health, and safety of the public (the basic tenet of all legislation) they would oppose the astute manipulation by tobacco entrepreneurs. Greatly increased taxation on tobacco products could provide the needed revenue for FDA (Food and Drug Administration) control over the constituents of tobacco as well as provide money for enforcement of laws governing the sale and use of tobacco products.

The concept of unrestricted "smokers' rights" is basically absurd. Is it logical that the smoker should have the right to light up at anytime, anywhere, and smoke in any amount? The **majority** of smokers do not even believe this. Even the tobacco industry's own 1978 Roper Report stated that the public favors political candidates who will take a position for control of smoking.

With the "make jobs at any cost" viewpoint of many legislators and the "sell products at any cost" attitude of tobacco purveyors, the consumer is caught in the web of aggressive, offensive, and injurious circumstance. The first step needed is for legislators to prohibit smoking at all main-body and committee meetings to clear the air and member's perspectives. Perhaps then, consumer attrition by the cigarette industry in particular can be de-escalated by a sensible and reasonable control over *all* forms of cigarettes and other harmful tobacco products.

Many government agencies are either regulating or selectively prohibiting smoking in their work places. Private industry is slowly coming around also to such a practicality. Legislation at state and federal levels, however, would solve innumerable problems for sensitive, ill, aged, infant, and child occupants of public space, buildings, and vehicles by definitive regulations that limit smoking in public and private places.

Legislation is needed at the national, state, and local levels that makes the purveyors of tobacco products legally liable for harm and injury caused by their use. Cigarette advertising in particular might be used as evidence that tobacco manufacturers imply greater safety in their low-tar, low-nicotine product. Such an impression is conveyed through their saturation advertising.

The public coffers and everyone's health would be benefitted by a substantive reduction in tobacco smoking. Millions of dollars can be derived at the state and national level that could be channeled into constructive use. Taxation calibrated to public hazard and risk could be legislated. Education has had little effect on youths who start the habit and the warning messages presumably directed to adults have had an almost imperceptible impact. Hitting people in the pocketbook is likely to be more productive, as well as benefitting their health, as the scale of their habit is reduced or it is eliminated.

Legislators should address the lack of control at the point of sale. Cigarette machines are open for business day and night to anyone at any age.

**thank you for
not smoking**

guidelines

As emphasized in this book, the least-expensive, most-practical, and most-protective measure is to prevent smoking by request, policy, or regulation with posted signs or symbols in indoor spaces. Alternatives may be more to smokers' liking but present innumerable problems in implementation. The goal is that everyone will one day be a nonsmoker.

The following guidelines are suggested as protective measures in the interim until the household or work place might be entirely free of any form of tobacco smoke.

- Have an open discussion with everyone participating.

- Discuss the effect of smoking upon smokers and non-smokers.

- Assure smokers and nonsmokers that they are valued and well regarded.

- Seek the cooperation of smokers for complete elimi-nation of smoking in shared spaces.

- Encourage smokers to cut down or quit (give moral support).

- Determine defined areas, rooms, or other spaces where smoking is not allowed.

- Provide separate, well-ventilated spaces for smoking.

- Separately zone the ventilation of nonsmoking from smoking areas.

- Keep any tobacco smoke from entering nonsmoking spaces.

- Provide energy-conserving, natural ventilation where possible.

- If smoking is allowed where nonsmokers are, place smokers downwind.

- Capture smoke with localized filtration or charged particles before it gets in mechanical systems.

- Provide outdoor terraces, patios, porticos, or porches for the smokers.

- Clearly define no-smoking spaces for visitors.

- Provide no ashtrays in no-smoking areas.

- In commercial places, supervise all cigarette machines.

- Use selective and activated-charcoal filters in central, mechanical systems.

- Use fireproofed and easily cleaned materials in any smoking space.

- In smoking spaces, use self-extinguishing ash receptacles.

- Separate ventilation for smoking spaces should be separately controlled.

- Provide rewards and gratifications for the smoker who quits.

i am a no-smoking cat

the last tribute

The cigarette is a tribute to the weakness of being human. It is the clearest statement of the universality that all life is transient and that we all will die. If we all thought that we could live forever, would anyone smoke?

Is smoking really that much of a pleasure or simply a route of addictive escape? The addicted mind of the hard-line smoker perceives that he or she may enjoy the habit, may feel surges of energy while smoking, and, possibly, be more productive. These addictive feelings, however, belie the reality. Smoking is a temporary stimulant; a volatile, health-robbing pastime; and, as many smokers state, a lousy, filthy habit. The cigarette is not a tribute to life; despite the glaring attempts of cigarette ads, it is a tribute to death. When smoking is a dead issue, no one will succumb to death from smoking.

glossary

activated charcoal (activated carbon) — a powdered or granular form of carbon made porous by special treatment, used as a filtering medium. Purifies by adsorption (adhesion to its internal surface).

addiction — a compulsive, physiological need for a habit-forming drug; discontinuance or decreased use of an addictive drug will cause physical symptons of withdrawal.

air change — the replacement of a quantity of air in a volume (room or building) within a given period of time. Usually expressed in air changes per hour (ACH). The average American home ACH rate is 0.5 to 1.5.

air exhaust — removal of air from a space through natural or forced (mechanical) means, usually to exchange "stale" air for cleaner, fresher air.

air tempering — heating or cooling incoming, outside air to condition it for use in a ventilation system.

air turbulence — departure in an air stream from a smooth flow, in which the velocity at a given point varies erratically in direction and magnitude. (compare laminar flow)

alpha radiation — a form of low-level, ionizing radiation. The specific alpha-radiation emitters in cigarette smoke are lead-210 and polonium-210, decay products of radon-226. Inhaled, insoluble alpha particles are difficult for the body to eliminate and accumulate in clusters in the lungs, bombarding delicate lung tissue with hot-spot doses of alpha radiation, which can alter chromosomes, cause cell mutations, and lead to tumor development.

atherosclerosis — hardening of the arteries, characterized by fat deposition on arterial walls.

bronchitis — acute or chronic inflammation of the bronchial tubes. Chronic bronchitis is often linked with pulmonary emphysema.

carbon monoxide (CO) — a colorless, odorless, toxic gas formed by the incomplete combustion of carbon; has an extremely high affinity for hemoglobin in the blood.

carcinogen — a cancer-causing agent.

cardiac — relating to the heart or heart disease.

cardiovascular — relating to or involving the heart and blood vessels.

cocarcinogens — agents that alone cannot cause cancer, but in combination with other chemical substances can lead to tumor development. Cocarcinogens enhance the tumor-producing effects of other chemicals.

convection — heat transfer by movement of a fluid (liquid, gas, or vapor) between the fluid and a surface or within the fluid itself.

convective air movement (natural convection) — a circulation of air due to difference in density resulting from temperature changes.

electrical potential — the capacity of a body or object to build up or respond to electrical charges.

electrostatic filter — a filtering device that removes dust from the air by inducing electrical charges on the dust particles.

emphysema — a lung disease in which the walls of the air sacs in the lungs break down, causing the air sacs to become larger and group together, reducing the total surface area for oxygen to be absorbed and trapping carbon dioxide-containing air inside the lungs; characterized by shortness of breath due to inability to expel air from the lungs.

filter medium — a substance used as a filter, such as activated charcoal.

gratification —	a source of satisfaction or pleasure.
hemoglobin —	an iron-containing protein pigment found in red blood cells that carries oxygen in the blood stream.
HEPA —	high efficiency particulate air.
inductive ventilation —	natural ventilation enhanced and induced through a rising air column generated by temperature differentials. If warm air is vented at a high exhaust outlet, cooler air from a low-level intake will flow into the space, replacing the warm air. This "stack effect" depends upon the temperature differential, the height between the inlet and outlet, and the size of the apertures.
infiltration —	the uncontrolled movement of outdoor air into the interior of a building through cracks around doors and windows or in walls, roofs, and floors.
ion —	an electrically charged atom or group of atoms caused by gain or loss of one or more electrons.
laminar flow —	a streamlined fluid flow in which all the layers of fluid move parallel to each other in a smooth path. (compare air turbulence)
lesion —	an abnormal change in the structure of an organ or body part due to injury or disease.
mainstream smoke —	tobacco smoke directly inhaled by the smoker from cigarette, cigar, or pipe and then exhaled. (compare side-stream smoke)
micron —	a unit of length equal to one-millionth of a meter.
mutagen —	a substance that tends to increase the frequency and extent of mutation (change in DNA structure).
natural ventilation —	supplying and removing air by natural means (such as by wind or natural convection) to or from any space.

negative ionization — introducing negative ions into a space, often for air cleaning purposes. Negative ions will attach to positively charged particles (which include most pollutants and cigarette smoke) and neutralize them or give them a negative charge, allowing the particles to be grounded or to be drawn to a positive electrostatic field. Negative ions are produced naturally by cosmic rays, radiation, the friction of moving water (causing the splitting of water molecules), and from needles on pine or fir trees.

negative ion generator — a machine that produces a stream of negative ions by means of the high-voltage corona discharge effect.

nicotine — a poisonous alkaloid ($C_{10}H_{14}N_2$) formerly used as an insecticide; the chief pharmacologic agent in tobacco smoke, a psychoactive drug similar to opium derivatives.

nitrosamines — cancer-causing chemicals formed by the chemical combination of nitrates and amines. Nicotine can permit the formulation of tobacco-specific N-nitrosamines which are potent carcinogens.

olifactory — relating to or connected with the sense of smell.

outgassing (off-gassing) — emission of gases and/or respirable particles; usually referring to emission of toxic contaminants from unstable synthetic materials, maintenance products, and finishes used in indoor environments.

ozone (O_3) — a triatomic form of oxygen formed naturally in the earth's upper atmosphere by photochemical reaction with ultraviolet radiation; can be toxic in certain concentrations.

particulate — referring to minute, separate particles or the particles themselves.

positive field (positive resonance) — a positively charged electrostatic field, used in conjunction with negative ionization to collect and ground out negatively charged particles.

precipitation — removing dust from the air by means of electric charges induced on the particles.

psychoactive — affecting the chemistry of the brain and nervous system, with resultant effect on the mind or behavior.

psychoneural — relating to or affecting the mind and nervous system.

radon — a radioactive gas formed by the disintegration of radium in soils; present in high concentration in soil gases and can enter homes through unpaved basements and crawl spaces and through wet and porous structural material. Certain building materials, such as brick, stone, plaster, sand, and gravel as well as well water may also contain radon.

radon "daughters" — radon gas decay products formed by disintegration of radon nuclei; several of these are alpha radiation emitters. Radon decay products attach to airborne particles, particularly on large smoke-tar particles.

return air — air returned from conditioned, heated, or refrigerated space.

selective filtration — choosing appropriate filter media to meet specific needs.

side-stream smoke (secondhand smoke, passive smoking) — tobacco smoke that goes directly into the air from the burning end of a cigar, cigarette, or pipe; not inhaled by the smoker. (compare mainstream smoke)

"smokeless" tobacco — snuff or chewing tobacco.

snuff — pulverized tobacco preparation that is inhaled, chewed , or placed against the gums.

stack effect (stack action) — see inductive ventilation.

tobacco —	various plants in the nightshade family, genus Nicotiana, cultivated for their leaves to be used for smoking, chewing, or as snuff.
toxin —	a poison.
tumor initiator —	an agent that renders a tissue suscept-ible to tumor formation.
vasoconstriction —	narrowing of the blood vessels.

references

American Cancer Society. *Dangers of Smoking — Benefits of Quitting & Relative Risks of Reduced Exposure.* Revised Edition. New York: American Cancer Society, Inc., 1980.

American Institute of Architects Research Corporation with Syska and Hennessey. *Energy Inform: Designing for Energy Conservation.* Washington, D.C.: AIA Research Corporation, 1978.

American Lung Association. *Second-Hand Smoke* (pamphlet). American Lung Association, 1982.

American Society of Heating, Refrigerating, and Air-Conditioning Engineers. *ASHRAE Handbook and Product Directory: 1977 Fundamentals.* New York, ASHRAE, 1978.

Bennett, William, "The Cigarette Century." *Science 80.* Sept.-Oct. 1980, pp. 37-43.

de Bono, Edward, ed. *Eureka! An Illustrated History of Inventions from the Wheel to the Computer.* New York: Holt, Rinehart and Winston, 1974.

Cahan, William G. "You've Come the Wrong Way, Baby!" Condensed from *Medical Tribune. Reader's Digest,* vol. 122, no. 732. April 1983, pp. 203-206.

Cenci, Louis. "Smoking and the Workplace." *Bulletin of the New York Academy of Medicine,* vol. 58, no. 5. June 1982, pp. 471-479.

Christen, Arden G. and Cooper, Kenneth H. *Strategic Withdrawal from Cigarette Smoking.* New York: American Cancer Society, Inc., 1979.

Cornell, George W. "Foes of Smoking Make Battle Religious Issue." *Denver Post* article, 1983.

"Ear Infection Linked to Cigarette Smoking." *Better Nutrition,* vol. 43, no. 6. June 1983, p. 6.

Gerras, Charles, ed. *The Encyclopedia of Common Diseases.* Emmaus, PA: Rodale Press, 1976.

Halper, Marilyn Snyder. *How to Stop Smoking.* New York: Holt, Rinehart and Winston, 1980.

Hamman, Richard F.; Barancik, Jerome I.; and Lilienfeld, Abraham M. "Patterns of Mortality in the Old Order Amish." *American Journal of Epidemiology,* vol. 114, no. 6. Dec. 1981, pp. 845-861.

Johnson, C.A. "Talk About Tobacco and Snuff." (magazine article)

Kunzendorf, Robert G. and Denney, Joseph. "Definitions of Personal Space: Smokers Versus Non-Smokers." *Psychological Reports,* vol. 50, no. 3, part 1. May 1981, pp. 24-29.

Malmsbury, Todd. "Eight Year Flats Study Says Plutonium Levels Normal." *Boulder Daily Camera* article. May 13, 1983.

Moran, Sarah E. "Smokers to Get New Habit-Kicking Gum." *Denver Post* article. September 12, 1983.

O'Rourke, John. "Smoke-Eyes." *Let's Live,* vol. 51, no. 6. June 1983, pp. 55-59.

Ott, Joseph K. " 'Soverane Weed' Artifacts Bewitch Tobaccomaniacs." *Denver Post* article. December 1978.

"Smoking and Deafness." *Better Nutrition,* vol. 42, no.12. Dec. 1982, p.6.

Stone, Irwin. *The Healing Factor: "Vitamin C" Against Disease.* New York: Grosset and Dunlap, 1972.

United States Department of Health and Human Services, Public Health Service, Office on Smoking and Health. *Smoking, Tobacco & Health: A Fact Book.* Washington, D.C.: United States Government Printing Office, 1981.

United States Department of Health and Human Services, Public Health Service, Office on Smoking and Health. *The Health Consequences of Smoking: Cancer.* Washington, D.C.: United States Government Printing Office, 1982.

United States Department of Health and Human Services, Public Health Service, Office on Smoking and Health. *The Health Consequences of Smoking: The Changing Cigarette.* Washington, D.C.: United States Government Printing Office, 1981.

Van, Jon. "Smoke Signals Teen Social Status." *Denver Post* article. April 12, 1983.

Weiss, William. "Smoking: Burning a Hole in the Balance Sheet." *Personnel Management,* vol.13, no. 5. May 1981, pp. 24-29.

"Why People Smoke Cigarettes." *Smoking and Health Review,* vol.13, no. 3. Washington, D.C.: Action on Smoking and Health, May 1983. Reprint of *Why People Smoke Cigarettes.* U.S. Dept. of Health and Human Services, Public Health Service, Office on Smoking and Health. (Washington, D.C.: U.S.G.P.O., 1983.)

additional sources of information on smoking and quitting

Smoking, Tobacco & Health: A Fact Book produced by the U.S. Department of Health and Human Services, publication number (PHS) 80-50150. Available from the Superintendent of Documents, U.S. Govt. Printing Office, Washington, D.C. 20402 (0-327-429: QL3)

Calling It Quits a pamphlet from the National Cancer Institute, National Institutes of Health (NIH Publication No. 79-1824)

National Interagency Council on Smoking and Health
419 Park Avenue South, Suite 1301
New York, NY 10016

Schick Laboratories
1901 Avenue of the Stars, Suite 1530
Los Angeles, CA 90067

5-day program on smoking aversion

SmokEnders
Memorial Parkway
Phillipsburg, NJ 08864

8-week program, check local phone directory for listing of local chapters

Office on Smoking and Health
U.S. Dept. of Health and Human Services
Public Health Service
1-58 Park Building
Rockville, MD 20857

Action on Smoking and Health (ASH)
2013 H St., N.W.
Washington, D.C. 20006

American Cancer Society
American Heart Association
American Lung Association
Seventh Day Adventist Church

check for local chapters

GASP of Colorado (Group to Alleviate Smoking Pollution)
12568 Maria Circle
Broomfield, CO 80020

check for other local GASP chapters throughout
the country

Californians for Nonsmoker's Rights (CNR)
2054 University Avenue, Suite 500
Berkeley, CA 94704

(415) 841-3032

This nonsmokers' rights group has assembled a five-les-
son supplementary curriculum, in cooperation with the
University of California at Berkeley, designed to accompany the anti-smoking documentary "Death in the West."
The film was produced in England in 1976 and depicts
six American cowboys dying of cigarette-related illnesses.
It was later suppressed by the Philip Morris Company,
makers of Marlboro cigarettes.

The "Death in the West" curriculum is intended for upper
elementary and junior high students and is designed to
maximize the educational and emotional impact of seeing
the documentary. The curriculum considers addiction;
the nature of tar, nicotine, and carbon monoxide; how
cigarette companies encourage young people between

the ages of 12 to 18 to start smoking; and, attempts by cigarette manufacturers to keep secret information about the health hazards of smoking.

Information about the curriculum and how to order a videocassette copy of "Death in the West" is available from the California Nonsmokers' Rights Foundation at the address above.

an architectural reference

Smoking relative to indoor air movement and the location where smoking may possibly occur are issues of architectural importance. The information and data contained in the book *Sun/Earth* (updated and enlarged edition), authored by Richard L. Crowther and published by Van Nostrand Reinhold, covers an optimization of solar, earth, air, and water energies for homes and buildings.

Chapter 10, "Use of Solar and Other Natural Energies," explores basic considerations of ventilation, natural air flows, sunspaces, greenhouses and atriums, as well as other natural energy aspects.

Chapter 12, "Holistic Energy Design Process," addresses the concepts, design resolutions, and total integrated (holistic) relevancies of human values with the site, architecture, and the interior. A holistic energy design process chart provides a framework for economic conservation design and biophysical well-being.

air cleaning devices

New Shelter magazine conducted tests in 1982 of small, room-type air cleaners to determine their efficiency in removing cigarette smoke.[1] Negative ion generators, fan/filter units, and one hybrid unit (combination ionizer and fan/filter) were tested. A small room (13ft. 4in. by 11ft. 8in. by 8ft. high, about 1200 cubic feet) was sealed and filled with the smoke from two unfiltered cigarettes and then the units were turned on. Each test continued four hours or until all the smoke was removed.

The results of the test found that negative ion generators were "distinctly more effective" at removing cigarette smoke than any of the fan/filter machines. The hybrid unit, a Bionaire 1000, was the most effective of all the units tested. Most of the fan/filter units produced very similar results.

---

[1]"A Test of Small Air Cleaners," *New Shelter*, vol. 3, no. 6. July/August 1982, pp. 48-57.

Although this test represents a comparative efficiency of air cleaning units, it does not represent in any manner the conditions that normally prevail. Usually more —generally many more— cigarettes are smoked during a four-hour period within such an indoor space. There is little substitute for appropriate ventilation, isolation, or appropriately designed nonsmoking areas.

sources of negative ion generators

(this list does not represent any kind of endorsement and is not a complete listing of manufacturers)

DEV Industries, Inc.
5721 Arapahoe Ave.
Boulder, CO. 80303

Ion Research Center
14670 Highway Nine
P.O. Box 905
Boulder Creek, CA 95006

ISI
940 Dwight Way
Berkeley, CA 94710

Zestron, Inc.
Dept. N-3
667 McGlincey Lane
Campbell, CA 95008

Bionaire, Inc.
P.O. Box 14
Paterson, NJ 07507

The Amcor Group, Ltd.
Empire State Building
Suite 1907
New York, NY 10118

HEPA units

Airomax
P.O. Box 86
Gibbstown, NJ 08027

Mason Engineering & Designing Corp.
242 W. Devon Ave.
Bensenville, IL 60106
(Cloud 9 Sterile-Aire)

Electrostatic air cleaners

Newtron Sales
3007 Lamar Blvd.
Austin, TX 78705
(This product develops a static charge as a result of air
flow without requiring electricity.)

a letter

weeding out smoking facts

by Trisha Flynn (article written for and published by the
                    Denver Post)

I smoke. I smoke a lot. The average smoker reportedly
smokes 11,633 cigarettes a year. I smoke more than that.

And it costs a small fortune. Not only are the cigarettes
expensive, but those little tubes of breath spray I buy to
keep my mouth from smelling like an ashtray cost $1.29
apiece. I go through about two a week. Then I spend
another couple of dollars on Windex to get all the yellow
gunk off my windows and pictures and mirrors and things.
And, of course, I have to buy room deodorizers so the
house doesn't smell like a stale cigarette butt.

Even though smoking is an expensive, filthy habit, I've
never seriously considered quitting. I am, in a word, addicted. Even though it is discoloring my teeth, aging my
skin, destroying my lungs, raising my blood pressure,
ruining my heart, clogging up all my vessels and stinking
up all my clothes. Even though my children despise it.
Even though I know I'm polluting their lungs as well as
my own.

where are the horror stories?

Just because I'm an addict doesn't mean I haven't been
frightened. A year ago a friend of mine died. He died of
lung cancer due to smoking. He was 39. He had two young
children. It was an awful way to die, not being able to get
enough air — constantly gasping and hoping. All he really
wanted was to hang on long enough to see his kids get
through grade school. He didn't make it.

A month ago a 59-year-old friend died because she smoked. Fifty-nine may not seem as tragic as 39. But it's every bit as tragic to her husband and seven children who just got through their first Christmas without her. It's doubly tragic when you consider that she would have had at least another 16 Christmases if she hadn't smoked.

It occurred to me that if I had known two people who had died because of smoking, then there must be thousands, maybe millions of others. So where are all the stories? Where are all the statistics? Why isn't this a bigger deal?

Well, I found out why. In the Wall Street Journal. And it's enough to enrage even a hardcore addict like me.

Ever since cigarette commercials were taken off TV, to-bacco companies have bought a disproportionate amount of newspaper and magazine advertising. The fact is, they outspend all other national advertisers in newspapers. So, of course, newspapers aren't exactly eager to print a story which bites the hand that feeds them. So many simply don't.

publications clear the air

In Minneapolis, for instance, a reporter covered a press conference announcing the Annual Kool Jazz Festival. When he wrote the story, he also inserted a list of jazz greats who had died of lung cancer. He was fired the next day.

A writer for "Savvy" was listed on the magazine's mast-head until they published her review of "The Ladykillers: Why Smoking is a Feminist Issue." Her name was subse-quently removed from the masthead because the publisher feared offending the cigarette advertisers.

In Harper's Bazaar, a woman wrote an article on the causes of cancer. It led off with smoking. The editor moved the smoking segment to the end of the article,

144

"so it wouldn't jump in the face of every cigarette advertiser." The policy still stands. In a recent story about health hazards in the office, three paragraphs on smoking were condensed into one.

And have you ever noticed that cigarette ads don't run near the obituaries? Or near news stories "antithetical" to smoking? If the publication goofs, the tobacco company is usually given an I.O.U. for a free ad at a later date.

Now, none of this is written down, of course. I mean the cigarette people don't walk into a place and fire employees or change content. The editors do that. The whole arrangement is sort of a Gentlemen's Agreement.

To be sure, this isn't happening in all newspapers and magazines. It's obviously not happening at the Wall Street Journal. But it is happening. And it's not going to stop. The tobacco industry spent $1.2 billion last year trying to hook people into a lifetime of buying their product. A product that slowly decays your body, pollutes the environment and kills people.

So I have a message for all you self-righteous, obnoxious anti-smokers: Keep it up. You may save us in spite of ourselves.

Reprinted with permission from the *Denver Post*, January 6, 1983.

a law

Minnesota has an enlightened law that prohibits smoking in all public and work places except in specifically designated areas. In regard to this 1975 law (the Minnesota Clean Indoor Air Act), C.B. Schneider, Section Chief of Environmental Field Services of the Minnesota Department of Health, has made the following written statements:[1]

"The MCIAA (Minnesota Clean Indoor Air Act) provides that a person who smokes in a nonsmoking area is guilty of a petty misdemeanor ... punishable in Minnesota by a fine of up to $100.

"The MCIAA also provides that '... the state commission of health, a local board of health, or any affected party may institute an action in any court with jurisdiction to enjoin repeated violations ...' The threat of seeking such an injunction has always brought compliance.

"In establishments which we license such as restaurants, resorts, hotels/motels, compliance with the MCIAA becomes one more of a number of health related items which are looked at during a routine inspection.

"Most of the complaints we presently receive deal with the work place. When a person complains about alleged non-compliance, we write a letter to the management of the work place indicating what their obligations are under the law. In a high percentage of instances, the situation (is) resolved through ... one telephone call.

"In general, it is my opinion that there has been broad acceptance of the law among employers.

"The most recent poll (May 1980) indicated that the MCIAA is approved by 92 percent of all Minnesota adults, including nonsmokers and smokers.

"I believe that the law has resulted in significant progress in protecting nonsmokers from ambient tobacco smoke at the work place, without an undue hardship on employers and smoking employees. *This has been achieved with minimum governmental intervention and at no additional public tax cost.*"

---

[1] Excerpts from letters written by C.B. Schneider, provided by GASP of Colorado. (Emphasis added)